# THE TALENT WAR

# THE
# TALENT
# WAR

## HOW SPECIAL OPERATIONS AND GREAT
## ORGANIZATIONS WIN ON TALENT

### MIKE SARRAILLE
### & GEORGE RANDLE

with JOSH COTTON, PhD

LIONCREST
PUBLISHING

THE TALENT WAR
*How Special Operations and Great Organizations Win on Talent*

ISBN   978-1-5445-1557-1   *Hardcover*
      978-1-5445-1556-4   *Paperback*
      978-1-5445-1558-8   *Audiobook*
      978-1-5445-1555-7   *Ebook*

*This book is dedicated to our families, friends, and a long list of military and business mentors who have helped shape and support us throughout our lives and careers.*

*More importantly, this is for those who have served, those who continue to serve, and those who have paid the ultimate sacrifice to protect our nation and our freedoms. You set the example for all Americans, and the business world has much to learn from you.*

*We will not forget. We will not fail you.*

# CONTENTS

# NOTE FROM THE AUTHORS

The Talent War is hard. There is no manual to follow. And there is no such thing as flawless execution in this endless fight. But with a few key principles and strategies, you can win this war and lead your organization to victory.

Both of us have dedicated our lives to talent acquisition and talent management in one form or another, and we've humbly and often embarrassingly made every mistake along the way. We know most military and business leaders probably share the same sentiments and same scars. This book is drawn from the many battles we have both won and lost during this war for talent.

Of eight hundred CEOs polled in 2019, the overwhelming majority of CEOs cited the ability to attract and retain quality workers as their top concern.[1] If you asked our senior military leaders in the Special Operations community, they would echo this same sentiment. It's all about talent.

---

1   The Conference Board, "In 2019, CEOs Are Most Concerned about Talent and a Recession," January 17, 2019, https://www.conference-board.org/pdf_free/press/Press%20Release%20--%20C-Suite%20Challenge%202019.pdf.

A company's dedication and commitment to fighting the war for talent is often the determining factor of success or failure, regardless of industry or domain. The only way to win is through trial and error, constant innovation, adaptation, and improvement of your talent acquisition and talent management procedures. There is no end state, no end to this war, just a steadfast commitment to engage in the fight every day, as the survival of your organization depends on it.

The Special Operations community has morphed into a world-class case study in talent acquisition and talent management. It's no surprise why the business world has developed a fascination with Special Operations Forces (SOF) and their ability to build winning teams—teams that often go against a numerically superior force yet find a way to achieve victory. SOF has become one of the most effective, innovative, and adaptive organizations in the world. They have effectively become a "talent magnet." Even so, they will admit they still get it wrong from time to time. What makes them stand apart is their constant evolution in their assessment and selection processes and their absolute refusal to accept mediocracy among their ranks.

We wrote this book because we believe the business world can learn a great deal from how SOF assesses and selects talent. We hope that business and HR leaders can utilize some of the principles used by SOF to strengthen their hiring practices. If we can prevent you from making the same mistakes we've made by honing your talent mindset and reevaluating your hiring practices, then we will consider this book a huge success.

Lastly, we want to highlight that we have taken every measure to protect the security of our brave Special Operations soldiers.

This book was reviewed and approved for release in cooperation with the Defense Office of Prepublication and Security Review (DOPSR). For this reason, you will notice that we do not delve into specifics about SOF tactics, procedures, or any other sensitive material. Instead, we focus on the high-level strategy that drives the SOF mindset toward talent. We do not feel as if this diminishes the book in any way, as it is the strategy and not the individual tactics that has truly led Special Operations to become one of the world's greatest incubators of talent. Throughout the book, we also share personal stories, including a few of our own embarrassing stories, and we have changed some names and details for the sake of privacy.

# FOREWORD

## by JOCKO WILLINK

Leadership is the most important thing on the battlefield—and the most important thing in business and in life. It is leadership that sets the example, it is leadership that makes decisions, it is leadership that unifies a team around a common goal, and it is leadership that takes care of the team and gets the mission done.

But one of the most important roles of a leader is often overlooked—the responsibility of building the team in the first place. The leader is responsible for training, equipping, and directing a team—but before any of that is possible, the leader must recruit, screen, and acquire the right people for the team.

Like many other leadership principles I followed in my career, I learned about the responsibility of a leader to build their team from the book *About Face*, by Colonel David Hackworth. Colonel Hackworth was a deeply respected soldier, battlefield commissioned during the Korean War, and decorated for valor time and time again. When he took over the 4th Battalion 39th Infantry

Regiment (4/39th) in Vietnam, he had his work cut out for him. The 4/39th was known in Vietnam as the "Hardluck" Battalion. They had a reputation not only for lacking discipline but also for suffering extensive casualties while rarely ever doing any damage to the enemy. Hackworth was personally selected to take over the battalion and fix it. And that is exactly what he did. He turned the "Hardluck" into "Hardcore."

But he didn't do it by himself. He brought the right people on board—he assembled a supporting cast of leaders that he knew would help him transform the battalion. Hackworth handpicked his battalion operations officer, who he had served with in the Tiger Force of the 1/327th and whose judgment and capabilities he respected. His Command Sergeant Major, Bob Press, was an outstanding enlisted leader who had served alongside Hackworth as a senior first sergeant at the 1/101st; Hackworth brought him on board to serve as the senior enlisted man of the 4/39th. Hackworth recruited Captain Dennis Foley to command Dagger Company; they had both also served in the Tiger Force with the 1/327th. He also recruited and brought over James Mukoyama, who Hackworth had known from his stint running a training battalion at Fort Lewis to be a company commander in the 4/39th.

These men and others formed the core group that led the turnaround of the 4/39th from "Hardluck" to "Hardcore." Clearly, it was not Colonel Hackworth alone that made it happen. He was certainly a force of leadership, but that force was multiplied by a decentralized command carried out through the leaders he had beneath him—leaders that he had recruited, acquired, and trained. Hackworth knew it is a leader's responsibility to build a winning team.

In the Special Operations community, this process has been developed and refined for more than a half-century. This process is still being honed, and it will never stop as it is required to secure victory from the hands of our future enemies. In the war for talent, there is no flawless victory, just a commitment to fight to win. The second you stop fighting, the second you think your process is perfect, is when you begin to lose.

I was an absolute beneficiary of the Special Operations recruiting, screening, and hiring process. During my last deployment in the SEAL teams, I was Task Unit Commander, leading two SEAL platoons in the Battle of Ramadi during the Global War on Terrorism. At the time, in the summer of 2006, Ramadi was the epicenter of the insurgency. A majority of the city was under insurgent control, and there were American soldiers and Marines wounded and killed on a daily basis.

I went to the battlefield with thirty-six SEAL Operators. One might think of all SEALS as mature, battle-tested, and highly experienced individuals. But that is not true. Roughly one-third of my SEALS had no combat experience whatsoever. They had never been overseas before, much less been in battle. But they all performed beyond anything that could have been expected of them. While some of their performance was certainly based on the training they received in the SEAL pipeline, their character as human beings was much more important than any training. In fact, were it not for the character these men possessed, they likely would not have volunteered for the SEAL teams in the first place and could not have made it through the assessment and selection process to become SEALS.

But they did—and it was evident in their actions. Men like Marc Lee, who fearlessly stepped into the line of enemy fire to protect his teammates. Men like Michael Monsoor, who smothered a grenade with his body to save his teammates. And men like Ryan Job, who boldly fought his wounds from an enemy sniper until the end. These young men—these heroes—sacrificed their lives for their country, their teammates, and their friends.

Where did these men come from? Yes, they were trained to operate machine guns, trained to patrol, trained to clear buildings. And yes, that training forged bonds between SEALs that cannot be denied.

But SEAL assessment, selection, and training—or any training for that matter—cannot create character where none exists. Yes, it can sharpen a person's will, increase their ability to handle stress, and teach them that they are capable of more than they know. But the raw material must be there. If an individual does not have the intrinsic qualities necessary, they must be weeded out. That is the primary function of basic Special Operations selection courses— not to train or teach students, but to find out which students have the minimum character traits required for them to be developed into high-performing team players.

These characteristics are present in a wide variety of people. From Ivy League graduates to high school dropouts. From kids raised in the ghetto to kids raised on farms. From varsity athletes to members of the chess club. A person's resume doesn't always reveal what lies underneath the surface. The Special Operations selection process does. It puts people into high-stress scenarios where there is nowhere to hide, where true character is revealed.

It is this process that differentiates Special Operations, and it is through this process that Special Operations has become a world-class organization any business would want to emulate. A focus on talent is at the root of everything Special Operations does. When you make a talent mindset the cornerstone of your organization, whether it's an elite military force or a business, you will always have the competitive advantage.

Of course, talent selection is not the be-all and end-all for winning. A team must foster a culture of solid leadership and continual individual improvement. People, especially highly screened and highly capable people, will not tolerate poor leadership—they will do their best to influence and change it. If they cannot, they will leave. We saw this in the SEAL teams and we see it in the corporate world. Bad leadership destroys the retention of good people. Good people will also leave if they are not encouraged and allowed to improve themselves—not only their skill level but also their level of responsibility. The best people want to be even better—successful organizations recognize that and provide those opportunities.

Developing a world-class hiring process is no easy task, but it is key to success. In *The Talent War*, Mike and George lay out the strategies that have made Special Operations so skilled at identifying and recruiting talent and explain how you can apply these same principles to your business. Mike and I served together in the SEALs, and I've worked professionally with both him and George. They have dedicated much of their lives to improving assessment and selection processes, and in this book, they share the most valuable lessons they've learned. With these lessons, you can improve your hiring process and get one step closer to victory. Because from the streets of Ramadi to the hundreds of companies I've worked with, while leadership is the most important thing on the battlefield, leadership is much more than just making decisions and unifying a team around a common goal and a plan to reach that goal. At the core of leading a team is a step that is too often neglected—the step of *building* a team. Without people, there is no leadership and there is no team. So, while leadership is the most important thing on the battlefield, the roots of leadership—and thereby victory—comes down to one thing: people.

The original Horse Soldiers from 5th Special Forces Group

*Source: Defense Visual Information Distribution Service / Maj. Melody Faulkenberry*

# INTRODUCTION

US Army Special Forces officer Perry Blackburn sat in the cold, dimly lit fuselage of an MH-47 Chinook. He had been tasked with a mission of strategic importance for our nation, and he was now midflight from Uzbekistan to Afghanistan. He was about to enter his first combat experience, and his mind was racing.

Perry's thoughts kept returning to his family and his wife, especially his wife's last words before he left: "Lead your men well."

Just weeks earlier, planes had flown into the World Trade Center and the Pentagon, launching the United States into its first war in more than a decade. The Global War on Terrorism would become the most significant combat action the US military had seen since the Vietnam War, nearly thirty years prior. And Perry and his troops—with the Fifth Special Forces Group (5th SFG), nicknamed "the Legion"—would be among the first US boots on the ground. A few brave men, all alone, unfamiliar with the terrain of Afghanistan and its people and outnumbered by enemy forces, would send a loud message to the world in the wake of one of our nation's largest tragedies.

The helicopter carried twelve of the best soldiers the United States Special Operations Command (USSOCOM) had to offer, thirty days of MRES (Meals, Ready to-Eat—bland but nutritional rations), and every piece of ammunition they could find. Major Perry Blackburn and his twelve Special Operations soldiers (called *operators* for short) had spent the last ninety-six hours in Uzbekistan, preparing for the insertion into Afghanistan to bring the fight to Al-Qaeda and the Taliban. They had been delaying the journey due to inclement weather, but they couldn't wait any longer. Though the flight would be difficult, they rebalanced the helicopter loads and took off.

Most pilots wouldn't even attempt the flight in those weather conditions, but the crew flying the MH-47 were part of the 160th Special Operations Aviation Regiment, known as "the Night Stalkers" or TF-160th. They were among the most skilled pilots in the world. If anyone could get Perry and his team safely to their drop point, it was these pilots.

Still, Perry kept close track of the helicopter's progress, planning what they would do if they were to crash here in the mountains. As his mind raced through strategy and tactics, he looked out over his operators. All of them were sleeping despite the helicopter's turbulence and the imminent combat operations. He wondered, not for the first time, *How did we manage to find these men?* These men of the US Army Special Forces (known colloquially as Green Berets) were selflessly willing to step into what the military refers to as a VUCA (volatility, uncertainty, complexity, and ambiguity) environment. These men had been highly screened and assessed for their capability to endure and overcome the most complex challenges our nation faces. Every last one of them was an incredible soldier who operated with the utmost skill and professionalism. They were the best of the best, and he would trust any of them with his life. He *was* trusting them with his life, just as they were trusting their lives to his command.

"We're over the mountains. Beginning descent," the pilot announced over Perry's headset.

The war was only just beginning. Perry and his men were the vanguard—the Tip of the Spear, as Special Operations Forces or USSOCOM are known. Their job was to pierce through the enemy's defenses and blaze the way for conventional forces, sending a clear and decisive message to the world in the process. Through television screens, the world would be watching this small group of men face a seemingly impossible task. But Perry blocked out the gravity of their mission and focused on the basics: *Just lead. Lead my men, lead them well, and our team will overcome any challenge thrown our way.*

---

Day after day, Perry watched his men adapt and overcome every obstacle placed in their way. They hadn't showered in weeks. They had to adopt unconventional tactics—namely, forming alliances with warlords in the region to build an Afghan fighting force. Because they were the first boots on the ground, infrastructure was nonexistent, and they were the only Americans in the Khost region, with the closest US forces located hours away. These twelve Green Berets would later be augmented with more US Army Special Forces operators as Perry built an alliance with his assigned warlord and raised a nine-hundred-man Afghan army that would fight

3

alongside the Americans. But for now, Perry and his men were truly on their own, where the slightest mistake could result in the annihilation of his team.

They faced other challenges too. They didn't have maps of the area, so they had to requisition and rely on old Russian maps for troop and ordnance deployments. At times, the rough terrain was inaccessible by vehicle, requiring the use of horses and mules, which would later earn them the nickname the "Horse Soldiers"—a nickname they are proud of to this day.

Despite the odds and the seemingly impossible task before them, the Legion was *winning*. They were forming alliances and securing ground from the enemy in the process. America was winning, through the efforts and actions of several dozen highly specialized and brave men. The US Special Operations community's greatest competitive advantage has always been its people. The Legion was composed of some of the most talented special operators in the world, led by the Army's best commanders, and the right people, led well and working as a team, can accomplish nearly anything.

---

Bullets snapped through the air as the Green Berets and Taliban exchanged fire. Dirt and shards of rocks rained down around Perry's operators. They were outnumbered, as usual, but they were better trained and more disciplined. While the Taliban's fire was chaotic, theirs was persistent and calculated. Slowly and surely, they were winning the firefight.

Suddenly, there was a loud crack and a blinding white flash. Perry was shoved forward, his gun flying from his hands. It felt as if somebody had hit him in the back of the head with a base-ball bat. Everything metal in the area rattled. He scrambled to his feet, beard sticking straight out on end. His first thought had been an enemy mortar of some kind, but as a rumble of thunder rolled across the sky, he realized that it had been a lightning strike. Perry was in utter disbelief. Of all the contingencies he'd planned for during the heat of the battle, getting struck by lightning had not made the list. On top of the Taliban, he would now have to fight Mother Nature too.

He checked the radio, which probably had attracted the light-ning to him in the first place. Nothing—not even static—greeted him. The sky had grown dark, and a deluge began. Within moments, the wadi (valley) was transformed into a flood zone. The ground was literally crumbling beneath their feet. All of Perry's men could swim, but some of their allied Afghan soldiers could not. Men slipped on the steep, muddy embankments, and a few were caught and swept away by the rapidly rising floodwaters.

*Oh Lord, is this how my command's going to end?* Perry thought. *Not in battle, but a natural disaster?*

Perry took a deep breath, calmed himself, and instantly switched gears, reprioritizing his efforts. They were no longer conduct-ing a combat mission. They were in survival mode. Fortunately, the enemy quit shooting and, having taken many causalities, also retreated to find cover from the downpour. Perry's team set up security and sent a group to recover the men being sucked down the wadi. Some of the men were spit out at the other end, beaten up from hitting jagged rocks, but they managed to pull everyone out, alive if not unscathed.

In unfamiliar, strange terrain against an inscrutable and difficult-to-identify enemy, and even in the face of the overpowering force of nature that no one could have predicted, Perry's men rose to the occasion, willing to win at all costs. Against all odds, they emerged victorious. It was a testament to the adaptive, high-performing teams the Special Operations community selects, trains, and continually develops to solve our nation's most dynamic national security affairs.

While Perry led his men well, they were the ones who executed the orders and, time and time again, secured victory. He had the best people, and that is the greatest competitive advantage you can have, whether facing an overwhelming Al-Qaeda force or a competitive business rival.

## THE KEY TO SUCCESS: YOUR PEOPLE

The operators of the Legion had few resources, little time to plan, and almost no infrastructure in the early days of the Global War on Terrorism in Afghanistan, so how did they manage to succeed where so many other military forces had failed? It was leadership—the people—the talented individuals like Perry and his operators. While he had far fewer men than the enemy forces, the *quality* of his men was far higher.

Leadership is the most powerful force in any organization. But leaders aren't a made-to-order product manufactured to specification. No, leaders are *people*. This means that the number one determinant between success and failure is *people*. It always has been and always will be. Wars are won and lost by leaders at every level—by the people, the human capital, that forms an organization. The Special Operations Forces (SOF) community has long recognized this fundamental truth that separates the SOF community from every other organization in the world.

The US SOF community is arguably one of the most adaptable, efficient, effective, and well-led organizations on the planet today because it prioritizes one thing above all else: *talent*. It spares no expense or effort during the assessment and selection of its people (what equates to a "hiring process" in the business world) and their development throughout their careers. On the battlefront, the difference between success and failure can mean the difference between life and death. With such high stakes, you need to be able to trust the soldier watching your back. The SOF community has developed one of the most effective talent assessment and selection processes to recruit those soldiers.

The business world can learn from how Special Operations recruits and develops talented individuals. In business, as in the military, the only competitive advantage you can hope to achieve and maintain is your human capital. *Nothing* is as important to your company's success as your people. Not your product. Not your service. *Your people.*

Blockbuster was once a behemoth but no longer exists. They failed to adapt to the rise of on-demand video, mail-order rental services, and automated kiosks like Redbox. Blockbuster even had a chance to purchase Netflix for $50 million but declined to do so, believing that their business model was sound and there was no need for innovation or change. Now, Blockbuster is a relic of the past, and Netflix is the Fortune 500 company.

Enron was named "America's Most Innovative Company" by *Forbes* for six consecutive years.[2] The service they provided was in high demand, and it seemed they would continue to thrive. Then the company was rocked by scandal due to ethics violations committed by its leaders.

Blockbuster and Enron believed their services and products were enough for them to succeed. People, however, make the choices that drive growth or trigger decline. Blockbuster didn't have leaders who could adapt, and Enron had the wrong leaders that made unethical decisions. The evident issue was a lack of leadership in these organizations. But the deeper issue was a lack of focus on hiring and placing the right leaders in the right positions.

Any good business leader will tell you that people are the most important factor in a business. Products and services come and go. If you want long-term, lasting success, you need leadership—and that means you need to select and invest in the right people. The who is almost always more important than the what. It's not what you sell that determines if your organization will be great; it's who you have doing it. People make the products. People deliver the service. People innovate and adapt. People solve the problems. And most important, people lead people to accomplish all these things. But despite knowing—or at least saying—that people are important, the vast majority of companies fail to attract and select quality talent.

Whether you realize it or not, you are currently in the middle of a war with your competitors: the war for the best talent. It is

2   Bethany McLean and Peter Elkind, "The Guiltiest Guys in the Room," CNN Money, July 5, 2006, https://money.cnn.com/2006/05/29/news/enron_guiltyest/.

the most important war you will fight within your business. And if you want to win, you need to commit to selecting and developing exceptional talent.

## DO YOU HAVE A TALENT PROBLEM?

Companies, like the military on a battlefield, can't afford underperformance. If your company is underperforming, you have a talent problem and are headed for failure.

Here are six signs that you have a talent problem:

1. **Sales** are down or stagnating, which means revenue is suffering.
2. **Labor efficiency** is abysmal, leading to high costs and wasted resources.
3. **Profits**, as a result of signs 1 and 2, aren't growing fast enough. Worse, they're declining.
4. **Customer satisfaction** is plummeting and resulting in customer and market share loss.
5. **Employee engagement/satisfaction** is declining because no one works as a **team**. As a result, **attrition** is rising, and the **culture** is becoming toxic.
6. **Innovation** is lacking or nonexistent. Individually and organizationally, there is no **growth mindset**.

The traditional business approach to talent acquisition, if left in the hands of unqualified practitioners, leads to bad hires. Companies often think that just because something works for them *some* of the time, it's good enough. It's not. Absent a talent mindset, your company will fail. We've worked with hundreds of companies, and we've seen it hundreds of times.

If, however, you get the right people, with the right mindset, and foster a culture of leadership, results will follow. Having the right people means greater profits, more satisfied customers, and better opportunities for innovation and growth. It doesn't mean you won't encounter problems, but with the right talent, those problems will be solved.

You need a well-planned and fundamentally sound talent acquisition strategy that will consistently result in quality hires.

If you've been using the same old, broken strategies, it's time to try a new method. Fortunately, there are Special Operations strategies and talent mindsets you can adopt and apply to your business that will let you retake the advantage and win the talent war.

## A BETTER APPROACH TO TALENT

Combined, the two of us have more than four decades of experience related to the assessment, selection, and retention of talent. We have both served in the military as well as in the business world, making our particular experience unique. Mike was a US Navy SEAL officer, enlisted Recon Marine, and Marine scout sniper. He assisted with the assessment, selection, and training of SEAL officers throughout his career. He is now CEO of EF Overwatch LLC, executive search firm and talent advisory firm specializing in the placement of Special Operations soldiers and seasoned military leaders in the private sector. George was a US Army officer and has spent two decades in corporate talent acquisition at the executive level across multiple industries.

We've been in the trenches, and we've seen the best—and worst—of both spheres. We have time-tested fundamentals in our tool kit, and with this book, we will share those principles with you.

In our years of experience, we've discovered that many organizations are really bad at hiring talent. The issues we see aren't isolated incidents but evidence of a deeper, systemic problem. On the most fundamental level, the majority of companies don't have a talent mindset, and it's holding them back. Yes, every CEO in this country will say they have a talent mindset and people are a strategic imperative, but few truly make talent a priority. If you are wondering if your company has a talent mindset, merely look at the overall performance of your company.

One of the biggest issues we've identified is that companies don't know what they're truly looking for in an employee; instead, they default to making hiring decisions based on past experience and how impressive someone's resume looks. We can't even count the number of times a company has gone against our recommendation and hired someone simply because they had industry experience, only to come back a few months later and say, "You were right. We should have hired the other applicant, who had all the hallmarks and attributes of a high performer." (As much as we like people telling us we're right, we'd much rather they hire the right people in the first place. And trust us, we are coming from a position of humility, as we, too, have made bad hires and beaten ourselves up over it.)

Even when companies know what they want in an ideal employee, they typically don't know how to attract that kind of person. And if they happen to stumble into good hires, they don't know how to retain them or help them achieve their full potential.

In this book, we will show you the effective hiring principles utilized by the Special Operations community to build world-class teams. Based on these principles, we'll show you how to identify what you want in your talent, how to attract and select the right people, and how to keep and cultivate your top performers.

## ORGANIZATION AND STRUCTURE

We've divided the book into three parts. The first part, "The War for Talent," lays the foundation of the book with a broad overview, including an explanation of what talent is and why a talent mindset is so important, as well as a discussion of what businesses, both large and small, get wrong when it comes to talent and what Special Operations does right in contrast.

In the second part, "Preparing for War," we outline the strategies that will set you up for success in the hiring process. We start by looking at the underlying strategy that should drive your assessment and selection: hiring for character and training for skill. We then outline the nine character traits of talent, followed by a discussion of why it's so important to assess your current employees and do workforce analysis to identify what you're truly looking for in new candidates. After that, we discuss how to attract the right talent, and finally, we explain how to build a good hiring team.

The third part, "Going to War," addresses how to select and retain talent. We delve into the hiring battlefield, with an emphasis on the interview process, and then cover the critical need for continuous training and mentoring of your employees to help them grow, both professionally and personally.

In creating this book, we interviewed over a dozen of the most talented people involved in assessment and selection, including military leaders, psychologists, CHROS, and CEOS, and their wisdom is interspersed throughout the book. We were also fortunate to benefit from the experience and wisdom of Dr. Josh Cotton. Dr. Cotton is a senior management consultant with a PhD in industrial-organizational psychology. He previously worked with the Navy SEALS and Green Berets to evolve their selection process, and now he works with businesses to help them identify and assess raw talent in similar ways. Dr. Cotton provided us with a psychologist's perspective, and his contributions have been invaluable to this book.

Whether you're a CEO, CHRO, executive, HR representative, mid-level manager, or anyone at all involved in hiring, you and your company can benefit from this book. The sooner you begin thinking about and approaching talent differently, the sooner you can begin maneuvering your team to win the talent war, so let's get started.

PART I

# THE WAR FOR TALENT

Special Forces candidates assigned to the US Army John F. Kennedy Special Warfare Center and School attempt to push a jeep through a muddy trail during Special Forces assessment and selection at Camp Mackall, North Carolina. Candidates who attended the three-week assessment and selection were evaluated on their ability to work individually and as a team.

*Source: Defense Visual Information Distribution Service / K. Kassens*

# CHAPTER 1

# A TALENT MINDSET

"You can't see talent," a Navy SEAL instructor told Dr. Josh Cotton. "It's not the biggest guy or the strongest or fastest. You have to *trust the process*. The process will reveal who has the potential to become a SEAL."

Dr. Cotton was working with the Navy SEAL community to improve their assessment and selection process. To that end, he had been asking all the instructors, "What do you look for in recruits?" He had received a lot of insightful answers: "people who don't quit," "team players who can also step up and lead," "resiliency," "people who are calm under pressure," "problem solvers." This was the first instructor who had taken the question literally, but it was a good answer. Because you can't inherently "see" talent, not in somebody's physical appearance and especially not on their resume.

Mike embarrassingly learned this lesson firsthand when he was a student going through Naval Special Warfare Basic Underwater Demolition/SEAL (BUD/S) training.

BUD/S, much like the training courses of other SOF communities, is more than just training; it's an intensive six-month assessment and selection process, with 80 to 85 percent of students dropping out before the end. BUD/S and other SOF courses are also unique in that officers and enlisted undergo the training alongside one another. The training evaluates how students lead, follow, and, most importantly, work as team players. Regardless of rank, all students are expected to lead and follow throughout the different stages of training.

Mike was a prior-enlisted Recon Marine (one of the Marine Corps' Special Operations–capable forces, which later became an official part of the Special Operations community in 2006) and scout sniper. In May 2003, he was discharged as a sergeant, commissioned as a naval officer, and issued immediate orders to BUD/S. Though he was newly commissioned, he was very much still a Marine sergeant with a roughneck style of leadership. There were several officers in his BUD/S class, including a few who outranked him, but the class gravitated toward and rallied around his style of aggressive leadership. The Marines had taught him how to lead a team, and he foolishly and arrogantly believed this naturally led to the ability to determine which candidates would make great SEALs and which candidates didn't deserve to be there. His six months in BUD/S would be a brutal lesson in humility and how wrong he was in his ideas about evaluating candidates. How could he be in a position to determine who would make a great Special Operations soldier when he was competing for the very honor the other students were striving for?

In this class, Mike made the same classic mistake that every business leader or HR manager makes when they toss a resume into the trash because the candidate doesn't have the exact education or industry experience required. Like most hiring managers today, he judged a book by its cover. That book was Ryan Job.

Ryan didn't look like a SEAL. He was on the heavier side—for a SEAL, at least—and nobody knew how he'd made it through the initial physical standards to even get into BUD/S. Mike looked at Ryan, and he made a snap judgment. *This guy's not going to make it*, he thought. Mike wasn't the only one who thought so. Much of the rest of the class and many of the SEAL instructors thought Ryan didn't fit the mold of a SEAL.

Since many expected Ryan to quit, the instructors decided to speed the process along. They threw everything they could at Ryan, within ethical and legal means, of course. BUD/S is already among the most intensive physical and mental training a person can endure, and it was even harder for Ryan. The instructors made him run extra miles and do more push-ups. They forced him to be cold, wet, and sandy longer than the rest of the students.

By the end of Hell Week, approximately two months into training, the class had gone from 250 students down to 35. Recruit after recruit rang the bell three times, signifying a DOR, "drop on request"—or in layman's terms, they quit. Only thirty-five guys were left, and Mike was one of them. He felt like he was truly part of an elite organization, a brotherhood. As he looked down the line of the physical beasts standing alongside him, he was astonished. A few candidates to his left stood none other than Ryan Job, who was smiling.

Mike and Ryan both reported to SEAL Team 3, and they eventually deployed together to Ramadi, Iraq, where they fought in the Battle of Ramadi in 2006, one of the fiercest battles during the Global War on Terror. Ryan performed exceptionally as an automatic weapons (machine gun) gunner during his days in Ramadi. After months of fierce fighting, Ryan was critically wounded during a major operation in south-central Ramadi, a contested area held by Al-Qaeda forces. He was shot in the face by a sniper while courageously laying down machine gun fire to cover a squad of SEALs closing on the enemy.

Days after Ryan was wounded, doctors declared he would never recover his sight. Insult to injury, he also lost his sense of smell and taste, but it didn't slow him down. After his injury, Ryan displayed the same drive and resiliency he demonstrated during his days at BUD/S. He refused to quit or feel sorry for himself. Despite all the setbacks, he finished his bachelor's in business with a 4.0 GPA. He ascended the 14,411 feet of Mount Rainier, and he even shot and killed a trophy bull elk. All without his sight, smell, or taste.

Ryan underwent countless surgeries and rehabilitation in the years after Ramadi. In 2009, only a few weeks after he found out he and his wife, his high school sweetheart, would be having a baby, he aspirated and died during his twenty-second surgery for his injuries. He became what SEALs call the "last fatality of the Battle of Ramadi." He was the third SEAL from his task unit to die. Fellow soldier Marc Lee was the first, and the second was Michael Monsoor, who was awarded the Medal of Honor for jumping on a grenade to save two SEALs, one of which was Mike Sarraille.

It's hard for Mike to believe now that he ever doubted Ryan. He was always waiting for a time to apologize, and he found that time while they were in Ramadi. After Mike apologized, Ryan said, "It's okay. Everyone's been misreading me all my life."

BUD/S attracts some of the highest-potential youth from across the nation, all highly intelligent, highly athletic, and highly motivated by the opportunity to prove themselves. Classes have included Ivy League graduates as well as NCAA and Olympic athletes. Classes have also included investment bankers and kids right out of high school who never played a sport in their life. Instructors have long since given up on predicting who will succeed and who won't because more often than not, they guess wrong. An elite athlete who can run farther and faster than everyone else has no greater chance of graduating than a former high school speech and debate member with "no quit" in him. The Special Operations assessment and selection processes destroy any previously held notions of what talent looks like.

The power of talent when you find it is undeniable, but talent may not look like what you think it will. Ryan didn't look the part of a SEAL. In the business world, he'd be the candidate with a resume that is immediately discarded. Fortunately, the Special Operations community has a talent mindset, and each branch's respective assessment and selection programs were built specifically to identify talent, not just people who *look* like talent. The instructors trusted the assessment and selection process, and they didn't eliminate Ryan from the training, giving him the chance to prove he had the attributes to succeed.

How many Ryan Jobs have you passed over for a job, simply because they didn't look like you thought they should? Talent will not and should not fit in a mold. You can't see talent on the surface;

you need a hiring methodology, like BUD/s or the other Special Operations schoolhouses, that reveals it. To create such a process, you must first reassess your definition of talent.

## WHAT IS TALENT?

At the most basic level, talent equals high-potential candidates—the people most likely to become high performers. Talent is people like Ryan Job. It is the individual who never gives up, who performs in high-pressure situations, and who will win when others say it's impossible. Talent is the leaders that make plans and decisions, and the people that drive teams forward. *And talent wins.*

Talent comes in many shapes and sizes. In an ideal world, you will have high performers at every level of your organization, from top to bottom. At different levels, high performers require different strengths and skills. A talented salesperson is going to look different from a talented software engineer, who is going to look different from a talented marketing director. Even within a single role, there is no prototypical "perfect candidate." To assume so spells disaster for any organization. If you want talent, you have to get rid of your preconceived notions about what the right candidate looks like.

For many companies, the number one factor in a hiring decision is the candidate's industry experience and hard skills. Though this may appear to be a sound strategy, it is exactly how you mistakenly eliminate talented candidates. As we will discuss further in chapter 4, "Hire for Character; Train for Skill," the best way to identify a high-potential candidate is to look deeper at *character*.

If you dissect the attributes that make a high-performing Special Operations soldier effective, you will find that they are the same attributes that make high performers successful in any industry. Talented individuals, regardless of domain expertise, share a common set of attributes. Based on our research and interviews, we have identified nine core characteristics that mark an individual as having high potential:

- **Drive**—the unrelenting need for achievement and constant self-improvement
- **Resiliency**—the ability to persevere in the face of challenge and bounce back from setbacks
- **Adaptability**—the ability to adjust according to the situation, learn new things, innovate, and try new methods
- **Humility**—self-confidence in one's ability while understanding that there's always room for improvement and that others' experiences and knowledge are valuable
- **Integrity**—an adherence to not only what is legal but also what is right
- **Effective intelligence**—the ability to apply one's knowledge to real-world scenarios
- **Team-ability**—the ability to function as part of a team, placing the success of the whole above the needs of the self
- **Curiosity**—a desire to explore the unknown and question the status quo in pursuit of better, more effective solutions
- **Emotional strength**—a positive attitude, high empathy, and control over one's emotions, especially in chaotic and stressful situations

These traits are heavily emphasized in Special Operations and explain why many veterans go on to accomplish incredible things in the business world after their military service. For instance, many companies—including Johnson & Johnson (Alex Gorsky), FedEx (Fred Smith), SoFi (Anthony Noto), Bridgewater (David McCormick), and 7-Eleven (Joe DePinto), to name a few—are run by veterans. These nine attributes are foundational to success, no matter the industry.

In the hiring process, you need to look for talent—those high-potential candidates who display the attributes and mindset necessary to become high performers within their respective fields. It's important to note, though, that a high-potential candidate does not guarantee a high performer. In BUD/S, for instance, the Honor Man, the top performer of the class, usually the most physically fit student, can often turn out to be an average SEAL. Until someone steps onto the battlefield, you never truly know how they will perform. Similarly, until a candidate begins working in their role, you cannot know for sure how they will perform.

While there are no guarantees, if you have the choice between a high-potential candidate and a low-potential candidate, obviously you are going to choose the high-potential candidate. The more high potentials you hire, the more high performers you can develop into effective leaders. The first step in hiring more high potentials is establishing a talent mindset.

## DO YOU HAVE A TALENT MINDSET?
## THE ULTIMATE LITMUS TEST

The strength of your alumni network is the ultimate talent-mindset litmus test. If your company is known for talent, then that will be reflected in the way your alumni are treated and in the way your alumni talk about your company.

When a company has a strong culture of talent, it has a greater proportion of talented employees, which means that alumni of the company are highly sought after. For instance, West Point, the United States Military Academy, is known for producing leaders, so being a West Point graduate can automatically grant access to numerous opportunities. A business corollary is McKinsey, which produces alumni that are statistically more likely to become successful business leaders in all industries. McKinsey is thus a rite of passage that can open up doors in life. While smaller companies are less likely to be known for talent on a national scale like West Point or McKinsey, they can still be known for talent within their communities.

How your alumni view your company is also a clear indicator of whether you have a talent mindset. The surest sign is if your alumni identify as members of your organization even after leaving. For instance, once you are a Marine, you're a Marine for life. When you work at a world-class organization that understands the power of people, it becomes part of your personal fabric, your DNA. If your organization becomes a part of someone's identity, it is the highest compliment and strong proof that you have a talent mindset and a reputation for good leadership and recurring success.

This part of the litmus test works with your current employees too. If they're at a party and someone asks them what they do, how are they going to respond? Are they going to say "I'm an IBMer" or "I'm a software engineer"? The former indicates a company with a talent mindset, while the latter indicates that your employees may not want to associate with your brand. If your company doesn't have large-scale brand recognition, your employees may not refer to themselves by company name, like "IBMer," but they will still mention the company and speak about it with pride.

## THE IMPORTANCE OF A TALENT MINDSET

"Everything's about talent," says Don Robertson, CHRO of Northwestern Mutual. "He who wins the war for talent wins the war."

Talent is what makes a company work. If you have the right talent, you have the ingredients to have the best company—the best leadership, the best culture, the best ideas, the best products. Nothing is more important to your organization than its talent. The only way to win the overall war is to have a core competency in your people, which means hiring, developing, and retaining talent. You can't do that without a *talent mindset.*

A talent mindset is the deep belief that leadership and human capital are the single most important competitive advantages your company can have. When a company has a talent mindset, assessing, selecting, and developing the best talent is a top priority.

> *Your human capital is the combined or aggregate stock of knowledge, competencies, leadership, and other attributes from your employees that produce victory.*

Many will argue that human capital is an intangible asset. You won't find it on your balance sheet or profit and loss statement, but it has more impact on your company and the bottom line than any other factor. And contrary to popular belief, it can be measured. It takes an adept business leader who has many hiring scars and talent battles under their belt to see it. Is your company successful and outpacing its competition? Then you are rich in talent. Is your company failing and being decimated by the competition? Then you lack a talent mindset.

After five years of research and study of hundreds of companies, McKinsey & Company consultants Ed Michaels, Helen Handfield-Jones, and Beth Axelrod identified a talent mindset as the starting point and most important factor in successful talent acquisition: "Building a better talent pool is not about building a better HR department. It's not about better training. It's not about extending the annual succession planning meeting from one to two days. It's not about offering more stock options. It is about leaders and managers at all levels embracing a *talent mindset*."[3] Where we differ from these authors is our belief that a talent mindset not only accounts for hiring talented people but also includes the continual development and investment in that talent through their tenure in the organization.

If you only take one thing away from this book, it should be the importance of a talent mindset. Effective talent acquisition exists only where there is a talent mindset in the organization. The only way you have true talent acquisition is if your leaders at all levels, starting from the top and going to the bottom, are aligned with the belief that managing your human capital is just as important as managing your financial capital. As Greg Case, CEO of AON, says, "People allocation is as powerful as financial allocation."[4] With strategic people allocation, you'll have the right people in place to manage the financial allocation and every other aspect of your business.

Most leaders will readily agree that talent is important. But saying something is always far easier than truly believing it and acting on it. A talent mindset is more than a general idea that people are important. It is a deeply held belief that sits at the core of an organization. It creates an organizational worldview, a way of seeing the world around you and interpreting what you see. It's reflected in the actions of an organization and is codified in its policies.

When a company has a talent mindset, the people side of business activities are not chores to be avoided; they are high-priority duties.

---

3    Ed Michaels, Helen Handfield-Jones, and Beth Axelrod, *The War for Talent* (Boston: Harvard Business School Press, 2001), 21–22. This book is an excellent resource. Unfortunately, the authors highlighted Enron as one of the model companies for talent acquisition and management.
4    Ram Charan, Dominic Barton, and Dennis Carey, *Talent Wins: The New Playbook for Putting People First* (Boston: Harvard Business Review Press, 2018), 19.

A talent mindset extends beyond theory to practice. In an organization with a talent mindset, leaders don't simply say that people are important; they show it through their actions every day. They put time and energy into creating a talent strategy, and they provide HR with the needed resources to implement the strategy. They design the hiring process to select high potentials—people with the character attributes needed to become high performers: drive, resiliency, adaptability, humility, integrity, effective intelligence, team-ability, curiosity, and emotional strength.

In any organization, whether it's the military, private business, or professional sports, talent makes all the difference in the world. To bring talented people into your organization, you must have a talent mindset. A lack of talent mindset is the most common issue we see in companies. In the next chapter, we will explore this and other talent acquisition mistakes that companies make.

## KEY TAKEAWAYS

- A talented individual is a high-potential candidate who displays the attributes and mindset necessary to become a high performer.
- A talent mindset is a deep belief that human capital is a company's most important asset—the only true competitive advantage that a company can hope to achieve and maintain.
- Where a talent mindset exists, talent is a priority, and when you prioritize and execute based on talent, you can't lose. When you win the war for talent, you win the war.

SEAL students assigned to Basic Underwater Demolition/seal (BUD/S) training compete as boat crews during the famed Hell Week. BUD/S has an average attrition rate of 75 percent. Coauthor Mike Sarraille is located at the front right of boat crew VI.

*Source: Mike Sarraille*

# CHAPTER 2

# WHAT'S SO WRONG WITH TRADITIONAL HIRING PRACTICES?

eorge felt as if he'd won the lottery for a career. Through a highly selective veteran hiring group, he had just been offered a position at one of the world's largest big-box retailers. According to a company representative, they were looking for driven leaders who knew how to mentor, lead, and provide vision for people. It sounded like a perfect fit for George. Plus, the job included a good salary, stock options, and growth opportunity. It was George's first civilian job after nearly a decade of active-duty service, and it would set him up to be able to go anywhere and do anything.

George accepted the job. His very first day of orientation, training, and onboarding was like a gut punch. Nothing was about talent or leadership. The position was none of the things they had advertised or told him. They didn't want a leader; they wanted someone who would fill vacant positions as quickly as possible with people who would adhere strictly to the rules. They were looking for cogs in a machine, not talent. Accordingly, their recruiting teams were evaluated based on efficiency—their speed of filling vacant roles and cost per hire.

To say it was a bad fit is a gross understatement. Nevertheless, George soon proved himself to be a high performer and was promoted. His new role still wasn't a good fit, so he applied for other positions within the company that he felt would be more suitable. Despite exceeding all his key performance indicators (KPIS) and being ranked in the top 5 percent of divisional employees, the company refused to move him. He was succeeding in a leadership role that others struggled with, so the company wanted to keep him there.

George made it twenty months before he quit. He wasn't the only one to leave quickly. Several peers who shared his talent mindset also left within two years. George and his peers had been able to transform and improve their small assigned corners of the company, but as soon as they left, everything reverted back to the status quo. Attrition went up, and all the critical KPIS went unmet.

George learned a lot of valuable lessons from that big-box retailer, primarily in what *not* to do, which can be as important as knowing what *to* do. It was a firsthand look at how broken traditional talent acquisition is.

The mistakes this organization made are the same ones we see companies make again and again:

- Lacking a talent mindset
- Not understanding how HR should be structured to drive impact
- Having a "butts-in-seats" mentality
- Participating in "fear-based" hiring
- Settling for mediocrity

Any one of these mistakes can spell disaster for an organization, but the most destructive mistake is a missing talent mindset.

## PEOPLE ARE YOUR MOST IMPORTANT ASSET

The enemy of greatness is a missing talent mindset. A lack of a talent mindset puts extreme downward pressure on a company's future talent, leadership, culture, and performance. When you see signs of a talent problem—like declines in sales, labor efficiency, profits, customer satisfaction, or employee engagement/satisfaction—they are small indicators of a much deeper problem. You have a sickness throughout the body, as it were.

If you want proof that most companies lack a talent mindset, look no further than the fact that CHROS are consistently the lowest paid of C-suite executives, sometimes being paid as little as one-third of their counterparts. CHROS have one of the most critical roles, if not *the* most critical role, after the CEO, in a company. They are the gatekeepers of talent. Yet most are not valued or empowered accordingly.

Most companies focus on the business side of things first—sales, research and development, and so on—and then if they have time, they work on the people side—talent acquisition and talent development. But if you want the business side to succeed, the people stuff must come first, because everything in the business relies on the people. "Whoever has the best team on the field wins the day," says Tracy Keogh, CHRO at Hewlett-Packard. No matter your industry, everything comes down to talent.

> *Building the muscle to hire great people*
> *is a competitive advantage.*
> —Patty McCord, the Chief Talent Officer
> of Netflix for fourteen years[5]

People are the most important asset. Good business leaders understand this to be a fundamental truth. The simple fact is that when you have high-performing people at every level of your organization, the organization performs at a much higher level. Yet so few companies go about talent acquisition and management the right way.

When a company has talent issues, everybody likes to blame HR. But it's not HR's fault—or not *just* HR's fault. If a company is struggling with talent, it's often because HR has not been empowered to win—has not been structured or resourced to be successful. That's a leadership issue.

In most companies, the CEOs say they want talent, but on a day-to-day basis, they do not dedicate any time or thought to talent

---

5   Patty McCord, *Powerful: Building a Culture of Freedom and Responsibility* (Silicon Guild, 2018), 74.

acquisition and development. They relinquish this key responsibility to others. Then they don't allocate the resources needed to build a successful talent pipeline.

A talent mindset starts at the top of an organization and filters down to every level. As CEO, you cannot delegate away your responsibility for talent acquisition. If your organization has a talent problem, it is up to you to own it. A hiring manager or HR representative can help establish a talent mindset, but for organization-wide change, the CEO and senior leadership must get on board too.

Think you have a talent mindset? If you say talent is important with words but fail to show it with actions, you don't have a talent mindset. If you say you want better people, but you don't allocate the needed time, money, and energy to talent acquisition and leadership development, you don't have a talent mindset. If you say you want "all-stars" but settle for mediocrity to fill a role quickly, you don't have a talent mindset, nor have you planned for success.

So now we will ask you again, do you *really* have a talent mindset at your organization? Because if you don't, the first step to fixing it is recognizing and taking ownership of the problem. And trust us—you *want* to fix it. The very survival and success of your company depend on it. It does not matter if you are a Fortune 500 or a new startup, talent will be the determining factor of success or failure, big or small.

## THE COST OF TALENT

When companies lack a talent mindset, it's a common refrain: cost. Creating a robust talent acquisition and management process is simply too costly, they say. What most companies don't understand is the major cost is not money, but time and devotion to creating a world-class talent acquisition pipeline. In the process, you will actually save money in the long run as your attrition lowers and you consistently make better hires.

The Special Operations community has long understood that *people are everything*. Special Operations soldiers go through three main stages: assessment and selection, training, and combat/war. The following table shows how those three SOF stages translate to the business world.

| Special Operations | Business |
| --- | --- |
| Assessment and selection | Talent acquisition or the hiring process |
| Training | Talent management and leadership development |
| Combat/war | Sales, marketing, production, etc. |

According to conventional wisdom, the first two rows of this table are non-revenue-generating functions. As such, many organizations spend as little as possible in these areas, viewing it as expense management, but not Special Operations. SOF has long invested heavily in assessment/selection and training because these two stages are what determine victory or defeat in combat. Essentially, investment in assessment/selection and training *is* an investment in effective combat units. You can't win a war if you don't properly assess, select, and train your soldiers. Without investment in the first two stages, people get hurt, fail, or, worse, die.

*Talent acquisition and talent management are indirectly the largest revenue generators because they impact every other revenue-generating function.*

Most companies operate on the principle of "revenue cures all." Everyone is concerned about revenue, and talent selection is often viewed simply as a non-revenue-producing function—a cost center. But much like the Special Operations schoolhouses that assess, select, and train future operators for operational SOF units, talent acquisition and talent management are what allow you to secure victory in sales, marketing, production, and every other department. Effective talent acquisition and management *do* cost money, but the expense is an investment in the future of your company, not a waste.

"Any investment in talent, in my mind, has unlimited potential," says Tom Lokar, former CHRO of Mitel. "There is an unlimited potential of return in human beings. You don't get that from a piece of equipment, you don't get that from a stock, you don't get that in a marketing plan."

Today, people are more important to businesses than ever. With growing automation and new technology, there has been a fundamental shift in companies' assets. "When you look at a P&L sheet, it's tough to quantify what portion of an organization's assets are human capital. Thirty years ago, 70 percent of a business's assets was probably equipment—trucks, buildings, machinery," explains retired US Army Special Forces Lieutenant Colonel (LTC) Brian Decker, former Commander of Special Forces Assessment and Selection (SFAS) and current Director of Player Development for the Indianapolis Colts. "Today, 80 percent of any company's assets is most likely what's between the ears of its employees. It's the human capital." If you've been neglecting talent acquisition and management, then you've been neglecting your company's largest asset and stunting your company's growth.

In addition to being your largest asset, your people—factoring in salaries, benefits, and so on—are probably your company's largest expense. If so much of your money is spent on people, don't you want to make sure that it is being spent wisely, on high-performing instead of mediocre employees? If you're going to spend $x$ dollars on salaries every year, the people earning those salaries might as well be standout high performers.

As your most important competitive advantage, your largest asset, and your biggest expense, *of course* human capital is going to cost you money, but the expense comes with a huge return on investment (ROI).

## THE ROI OF TALENT ACQUISITION

Talent acquisition can carry a huge return on investment (ROI), both tangible and intangible. For instance, say it costs $10,000 (to cover administrative costs, assessment tests, background checks, and so on) to hire an incredible salesperson. In the first year, the salesperson closes 50 percent more sales than the average salesperson, generating a tangible return on investment for the organization. An even greater, intangible return on investment is the impact that incredible salesperson can have by leading and mentoring the salespeople around him or her, elevating the performance of the overall team and leading to a greater overall return.

Sometimes the ROI won't be as clear. Maybe you hire a talented software engineer who builds a new tool to improve the customer experience, or maybe you hire a leader who creates a happier, healthier work culture. You may not be able to assign an exact dollar amount to those hires' impact, but they are helping your company to innovate and compete—that's the most important ROI. If you don't believe us, just look at Google. As a proportion of its people budget, Google spends *twice* as much as its competitors to find the best people.[6] Google invests in talent because that is how you win the war in business.

For businesses, one of the highest avoidable costs is attrition, and investing in talent acquisition and management can lower your attrition rates. According to a Center for American Progress study, the average cost of replacing an employee in a midrange position (earning $30,000 to $50,000 a year) is 20 percent of their annual salary. So replacing a manager making $40,000 a year would cost $8,000. For senior-level executive positions, the cost can climb to 213 percent of the individual's annual salary, meaning the cost to replace a $300,000-salary CEO could be as great as $639,000.[7] If attrition in your company is 20 percent, you could easily be bleeding millions of dollars.

Attrition also carries a frequently overlooked cost in terms of lost productivity. It can take months or even years for a new

---

6   Kim Pope, "Is Your Talent Acquisition a Revenue Generator?" WilsonHCG, July 18, 2018, https://www.wilsonhcg.com/blog/is-your-talent-acquisition-a-revenue-generator.

7   Heather Boushey and Sarah Jane Glynn, "There Are Significant Business Costs to Replacing Employees," Center for American Progress, November 16, 2012, https://www.americanprogress.org/wp-content/uploads/2012/11/CostofTurnover.pdf.

employee to complete onboarding and begin contributing to the company in a meaningful way. Even if you're able to fill a role quickly, at minimal cost, and with a rapid onboarding, the team will be damaged by that attrition. As Joe DePinto, CEO of 7-Eleven, points out, "Whenever one person comes out of a team and a new person comes in, the team dynamic starts all over again." Every time a team's makeup changes, it takes time for the team to establish a new dynamic and perform at its most effective.

Investment in talent also leads to more homegrown talent, which offers more cost savings. When it comes time for a leader to move out of their seat, you don't have to invest as much in attracting outside talent, because you already have qualified people inside your organization. With a proper talent strategy, the majority of your promotions will be internal, and internal hires are significantly cheaper and more effective than external ones, as you do not have to spend money attracting talent, running background checks, and completing any number of administrative tasks.

In the long run, hiring the wrong people will cost you more money than you'll save by skimping on talent acquisition. On the other hand, hiring the *right* people will bring outsize returns. So yes, there is a cost, and it's well worth it.

If cost isn't what's holding you back in talent acquisition and management, the issue may be a fundamental misconception about what HR is meant to do.

## HR LEADERS MUST BE BUSINESS LEADERS

Patty McCord, in her book *Powerful*, says, "Your HR people *must be* business people."[8] Tracy Keogh, one of the most skilled and effective CHROS in the world today, is an excellent example of what McCord means.

Before settling her career trajectory on an HR path, Tracy worked as a hospital administrator on a divisional level for seven years, a management consultant for five years, and a director of operations for an IT consulting firm.

At that IT consulting firm, when the head of HR quit, the CEO asked Tracy if she wanted to run HR. She said no. She told him the HR department was too broken and outlined a few of the things that needed to change. "You got the job," he told her, recognizing that Tracy's business-focused approach was exactly what their HR department needed.

After leaving HR for a short stint in sales and marketing, Tracy returned to HR, moving from company to company until she ultimately ended up as head of HR at Hewlett-Packard.

---

8   Patty McCord, *Powerful: Building a Culture of Freedom and Responsibility* (Silicon Guild, 2018), 104.

Because her background was not originally in HR, Tracy brought a unique, more strategic leadership perspective to her CHRO role. "I've worked in all parts of the business," Tracy says, "and to me, the most important lever is people, but most business-oriented people don't consider going into HR, even though HR is at the center of all decision-making for the organization."

When you put high-performing business leaders like Tracy into HR, you can transform the department into a powerful, strategic function within the company. HR people with strong business acumen understand the company's goals and challenges, and they understand the teams and personalities they support. They understand sales cycles, product development timelines, and milestones, and many know how to evaluate the deep technical skills needed in today's ever-evolving companies. With this more holistic view of the business, they have a better understanding of the talent needed to drive the business toward success.

## HUMAN RESOURCES— OVERHEAD, COMPLIANCE, OR STRATEGIC FUNCTION?

Shortly after Tracy Keogh stepped into her role as CHRO at Hewlett-Packard, a C-suite meeting was called to discuss strategy. At the meeting, one of the other executives told Tracy, "I'm glad HR is at the table."

While the executive likely made the statement in jest, it was undoubtedly a jab at HR, as if the executive was *surprised* that HR should be involved in setting the company's strategy. A testament to Tracy, she smirked and quickly fired back, "We *are* the table." The surrounding executives never questioned the importance of HR again.

Human resources is as foundational to the success of your company as any other function, but few business leaders truly know how to properly use their HR department, and most HR departments either don't know what right looks like or are poorly led.

Philosophically, in companies where HR is seen as a non-revenue-generating function, HR departments are set up to be administrative instead of strategic. Instead of working to strategically build and grow talent in the organization, their only job is to complete personnel tasks such as pay and benefits and protect the company from legal liability. Tracy gave us an easy rule of thumb to determine what function your HR department is playing: "If HR reports into finance, it's an overhead function, if it reports into legal, it's a compliance function, and if it reports into the CEO, there's a prayer that it'll be a strategic function."

Many companies have a fundamental misalignment between upper leadership and HR, where leadership says they want talent, but HR is not set up to actually hire for talent. In fact, HR often doesn't even know what talent looks like in the company. There is no gold standard of talent. Instead, hiring is a mechanical, order-taking process based on objective requirements. Leadership gives HR a laundry list of what they want—years of experience, required skillset, and compensation range—and HR goes out and fills the order.

To have effective talent acquisition, your business leaders and HR department must be strategic partners. The talent acquisition team must be "students of the business," understanding the organization's underlying goals and the talent needed to achieve them. "Since day one in my career," Joe DePinto told us, "I have always had my CHRO linked at the hip and will continue to." As Joe has discovered, to function strategically, your HR department must be part of the planning process for both talent acquisition and management. HR should be involved in succession planning and gap analysis to assess, select, and develop talent in a strategic way.

Neither HR nor upper-level leadership is entirely to blame for the disconnect in what HR is supposed to be. HR isn't getting the needed direction, and upper-level leadership have likely never seen HR function the way it should, so they don't understand the impact it could have as a strategic function.

Both HR and leadership are responsible for transforming HR into a strategic function. On the leadership side, you need to equip your HR department with the needed resources and work with them to ensure that your talent acquisition tactics are aligned with your talent strategy. On the HR side, "You have to educate your leadership on how to engage with you strategically," Tracy says. "You also have to take the business problems your leadership has and translate them into people solutions. That's not their job; that's HR's job."

If your leadership and HR department are not aligned, it could be because you are measuring and incentivizing the wrong metrics related to hiring.

## RECRUITING VERSUS TALENT ACQUISITION

In hiring, there is a big difference between *recruiting (or staffing)* and *talent acquisition*.

With recruiting, hiring is reactionary. You are trying to fill vacant positions as quickly as possible. There is a very short-term mindset. HR is not part of the planning process and simply executes the orders it receives from leadership.

With talent acquisition, you are seeking talent as an investment in your long-term human capital. Instead of trying to fill seats quickly, you are focused on the long game and working to fill seats with the right people. Your recruiters are "talent consultants" who are students of the business they support and experts in the talent marketplace. Talent acquisition becomes a team sport, with HR and leadership working together to create a strategic plan for hiring to support the growth of the company.

## BUTTS-IN-SEATS MENTALITY

"Probably the biggest fault of selection is impatience," says Tom Lokar. "There is a pressure to fill that job and get someone in the seat."

*When you weight time constraints over following good hiring practices, you've already compromised the process.*

Companies always say they want talent, but when they measure the effectiveness of their hiring process, none of the metrics are related to quality hires. Instead, HR departments are evaluated based on efficiency—the speed of filling vacant roles and cost per hire, just as George was evaluated at the big-box retailer. Because HR isn't traditionally seen as a revenue-producing function, companies want it to operate as efficiently as possible, even if that efficiency comes at the cost of lower-quality hires.

What gets measured gets done. If you measure based on efficiency, you will create what we call a *butts-in-seats mentality*, where all that matters is filling a role with a warm body. We aren't saying efficiency isn't important. Efficiency at the cost of effectiveness is the problem. When you create and execute a thorough hiring process, knowing exactly what you're looking for, much like the Special Operations community, your process becomes both more efficient and more effective with each new hire.

Working in talent acquisition, George has dealt with the butts-in-seats mentality many times. In his biggest year, he hired more than twenty thousand people. While it *is* possible to hire in quantity without sacrificing quality, it is extremely challenging, especially if you are measuring efficiency and enforcing tight timelines.

That is exactly the situation George encountered while working at an information technology company. Cybersecurity was becoming an increasingly relevant issue, and the company decided to create a new and separate enterprise-security division of eight hundred people. They chose the leader and built a go-to-market plan, complete with revenue strategies and estimations. They even went to HR to work out compensation and benefits. The senior leadership was thrilled, thinking they had a well-thought-out, strategically planned, billion-dollar idea.

When George was finally invited into the planning process, it was mid-May, and they were projecting revenue for Q1 of the next year for an eight-hundred-person division that did not exist. George then asked the critical question that had been overlooked: "Who is going to make up this division?" While the leadership had consulted with HR to figure out the administrative portion of salaries and benefits, they had not created a strategic plan for how to acquire the talent.

The senior leadership told George that they were projecting about seven hundred external hires. In just seven months, George was supposed to hire seven hundred people, onboard them, and produce revenue. Not once had anybody questioned how difficult this would be. They simply assumed it would happen, treating it as if they were ordering products off the shelf from Amazon. The problem is these were humans, not products, and humans get a say in everything they do.

The timeline was so aggressive that George had to pull approximately 150 recruiters from their normal workload and throw them against this one recruiting effort. Even with the extra manpower, they had to operate at Mach 2 speed for all seven months. All told, they spent about $1 million in agency fees, which meant the division would be starting out $1 million in the red before they could start accruing profit.

But they did it. Despite having no plan, not enough time, and a hard sell convincing people to take a chance on a brand-new division, they hired seven hundred people.

This might sound like a success story, but the story doesn't end here. Even though they were able to hire seven hundred people, they hadn't been given the time to undergo a process that truly evaluates high-potential talent. The hired team was not able to generate the revenue predicted, and within nine months, attrition had climbed to 30 percent. Additionally, because George had to pull 150 of his recruiters away from their normal duties, vulnerabilities had grown in other parts of the company.

Between quantity, quality, and speed, you can reasonably expect to accomplish two of the three. You can have quantity and quality but not speed, quality and speed but not quantity, or, what most companies choose: quantity and speed but not quality.

Most HR departments do not measure anything that identifies whether their hiring tactics actually work to hire *talent*. If you want to hire talent, then your HR department shouldn't be incentivized based on their number of hires and speed of hiring. They should be incentivized by how well those hires do in the roles. That requires a feedback loop that analyzes the success or failure of each hire and connects it back to what occurred in the hiring process. Without this feedback loop, nobody is rewarded *or* held accountable for hiring talent.

## AN ALL-TOO-COMMON STORY: HR "ORDER TAKERS"

After George was recruited from a top consulting firm to take over the Americas region for one of the world's largest tech firms, it only took the first twenty-four hours for him to see he had a big problem. He had thirty-three recruiters in his department who served as functional "order takers," with twenty-five or more hiring managers each to connect with and, on average, sixty-five open positions per recruiter, multiplied by forty to fifty applicants per role. You can do the math—this was a volume and speed play.

If that wasn't complex enough, these positions were scattered across multiple business units and involved multiple countries and associated employment laws. Plus, half of the thirty-three recruiters had been employed less than nine months, and the ones with tenure were contract recruiters. Their hiring wasn't strategic; it was simply survival.

The root cause of this scenario was not apparent to most, being easily camouflaged by the complexity and size of the firm. Two years earlier, the company had acquired a large IT services organization to complement its product offerings. In the acquisition and assimilation period, it was determined that the main company had sufficient internal recruiting resources,

49

thereby making many of the incoming resources from the acquired firm redundant. Further, both HR and recruitment were afterthoughts from a strategic perspective. Their input to the future talent needs of the combined firms was never solicited, which resulted in the top leadership missing the critical fact that the two companies operated in different environments, requiring talent acquisition to operate differently. The acquired company, a 135,000-person firm, had a heavy focus on customer-facing work and consultations. Because it spent most of its time externally focused on clients, it required a more robust behavioral interviewing approach than a product company would need.

But George's department hadn't been equipped to adopt the needed talent acquisition approach. Instead, it was about getting "butts in seats," as fast as they could.

The downstream effect was easily seen in higher attrition, lower sales, lower renewals rate, employee engagement challenges, and increased need for leadership development—eventually creating a vicious circle.

The solution, as Jocko Willink would say, was "simple, not easy." With an aggressive, proactive approach, George managed to turn the department around, but it was complex and time-consuming. It took him nearly eighteen months to shift the hiring focus from speed to hiring the best talent. This involved quadrupling the number of recruiting resources, increasing the talent and labor budget, changing processes and tools, and hiring trained and experienced full-lifecycle talent consultants (recruiters who are involved in the entire process, from sourcing and attracting talent to screening, interviewing, and negotiating offers). Slowly but surely, the recruiters transitioned from "order takers" to strategic partners in building the company's greatest advantage: people.

## FEAR-BASED HIRING

The Special Operations community has become a world-class model for *potential-based* hiring, which is the foundation of their assessment and selection process. In contrast, many companies, instead of hiring the candidates with the most potential, hire those candidates that inspire the least amount of fear. This kind of fear-based hiring usually comes down to one of three fallacies:

1. Red flags are more important than green flags.
2. Leaders shouldn't be outshined by their followers.
3. Somebody is better than nobody.

### RED FLAGS ARE MORE IMPORTANT THAN GREEN FLAGS

In traditional corporate hiring practices, the objective has seemingly shifted from "hiring the best" to "hiring the familiar and safe." People are more afraid of a bad hire than they're excited by a good hire.

To an extent, this fear is understandable. With a single individual, you can't hire your way to success, but you can hire your way to destruction. If you hire a talented employee and stick them in a bad company, there's only so much they can do to improve the status quo. But if you hire a bad employee into a good company, they can wreak havoc with poor performance and ethics violations, poison a good culture, or disrupt the team dynamic.

So once applications pour in, instead of searching for talent, many companies search for bad candidates to weed out of the pool. They assume that if they focus on getting rid of applicants, whatever they're left with will be the best choice. It makes sense theoretically, but in practice, the best talent is often thrown out. Hiring managers become hypersensitive to negative information until they see red flags everywhere. Misspelling on the cover letter? Application in the trash. Applicant doesn't have a 3.5 or higher GPA? In the trash. Applicant has ten years' leadership experience in the military but no prior industry experience? In the trash.

If you're focused on screening people out instead of screening people *in*, you can easily miss out on the best talent, especially because signs of greatness can sometimes show up as red flags. When a high-potential candidate shows up and all you hire is the adequate, that candidate will look very different. Different is misread as a red flag, so your high-potential candidate's resume goes where? In the trash.

Fear-based hiring is dogmatic about *objective* requirements. Black-and-white criteria make it easy to say yes or no. Does this person have $x$ years of industry experience? Does this person have $y$ degree? These criteria don't matter nearly as much as you might think. LTC Brian Decker, former Commander of Army Special Forces Assessment and Selection, told us, "When I arrived at my command, anything easily measured was heavily weighted in the selection process. The problem was it didn't have a lot of predictive value." The same is true in business. Just because you can measure something doesn't mean it's important, and just because you can't measure it doesn't mean it's not important.

The only question that truly matters is "Does this person have the potential to be a top performer?"

Don't disregard red flags entirely, but don't obsess over them either. In combat, you don't want to get shot. But at the same time, if your *primary* concern is not getting shot, then you don't go into battle. If you make your hiring decisions based on avoiding your worst-case scenario, then you will never achieve your *best-case* scenario. It is far more effective to look for green flags than red flags.

## LEADERS SHOULDN'T BE OUTSHINED BY THEIR FOLLOWERS

Average or underperforming managers often fear hiring somebody who will outshine them, because they don't want to hire themselves out of a job.

There should never be a maximum standard for talent, only a minimum. If you're not hiring people better than your current employees, you will never raise the bar for talent within your organization.

There are two ways to counteract this fallacy. The first is to choose your hiring team carefully. As we will discuss further in chapter 8, "Build Your Hiring Team," A-players choose other A-players, while B-players and C-players are more likely to fear choosing someone better than them. Special Operations places only their A-players, with the humility to recognize high-potential candidates who could be better than them, into the assessment and selection instructor positions.

Another solution is to create a quantitative assessment of talent and require that new talent exceeds current talent. Some companies assess different attributes of their current talent on a number scale and then assess candidates on the same scale. They only hire people who score higher than the average. If the average employee scored six out of ten on leadership, only candidates scoring seven or higher would be hired.

## SOMEBODY IS BETTER THAN NOBODY

Because of a butts-in-seats mentality, a lot of companies would rather fill a seat with a mediocre hire than report upward that they're short people on the team.

A vacant position is hard on the entire team. Everyone else must pick up the slack, and in lean companies, teams are sure to fall behind on their goals and timelines if they're not properly staffed. You *should* fill a vacant position as quickly as possible, *but only with talent.* Special Operations Forces almost always have fewer operators than their authorized allowances, yet these small teams continue to outperform larger organizations. Why? Because the SOF community refuses to compromise standards to increase their numbers. *It's not an option.*

Nobody is better than just anybody. An empty position creates short-term problems, but a bad or mediocre hire can have long-lasting ramifications.

## SETTLING FOR MEDIOCRITY

A lot of companies take an "If it ain't broke, don't fix it" attitude toward talent. "You'll never move ahead with that attitude," says Lieutenant General William Boykin, three-star general and former commander of a highly selective and specialized Army Special Operations unit, the US Army Special Operations Command (USASOC), and the US Army John F. Kennedy Special Warfare Center. "It means you want to maintain the status quo." If you're accepting mediocrity, then your talent acquisition program *is* broken, and it needs to be fixed.

Companies are too content being average. If employees are ranked on a scale of one to five, the ideal for most companies is to have the bulk of their people land on a three. As long as an individual is doing better than the *worst* employees, then they're classified as a "good" employee. Could you imagine if the Special Operations community adopted a "good enough" approach toward talent? They wouldn't be nearly as capable and effective. ISIS leader Abu Bakr al-Baghdadi and Al-Qaeda leader Osama bin Laden would still be alive, and Captain Phillips would never have been rescued from the gravest of circumstances. Essentially, Special Operations would no longer be "special."

"Good" isn't good enough. *Great* is what will get you results. Great is what will give you a competitive advantage. Great wins.

The Pareto principle states that 80 percent of effects come from 20 percent of causes. In terms of talent, this means that 80 percent of your positive outcomes come from the top 20 percent of your talent, and 80 percent of your negative outcomes come from your bottom 20 percent. Traditional advice thus tells you to focus your attention on your top and bottom 20 percent of employees.

In some circumstances, this is sound advice, but the issue is that this principle has been warped to mean that the mathematical distribution of your employees should be 20 percent high performers at the top (A-players), 60 percent average employees in the middle (B-players), and 20 percent low performers at the bottom (C-players). Within a group of ten A-players, some people will still fall at the top and some at the bottom. However, *relative to the universe*, they are all still A-players. Relative to your company, it is okay to have 60 percent of your employees fall in the middle, but relative to the wider world, your average should translate to A-player.

The acceptance of mediocrity extends beyond current employees to new hires. Terminating employees can be a difficult and lengthy process, making it even more important to guard the initial gate into your company. There is no excuse for hiring a person you know to be mediocre. Saying no to a candidate is far easier and less expensive than letting them become a poor performer who must be terminated.

When you're filling a position, if all you can find is mediocrity, then *keep looking*. Finding great talent means not having artificial timelines attached to hires. This is an endless war that companies must be prepared to fight to win.

Special Operations Forces do not accept mediocrity. It is part of the SOF ethos, the very fabric that makes SOF such an effective and elite organization. In the next chapter, we'll take a closer look at how SOF succeeds with talent where many companies struggle or fail.

# KEY TAKEAWAYS

- A missing talent mindset is the number one mistake companies make when it comes to building a world-class organization. Having a talent mindset throughout your organization is the first step to winning the talent war.
- Your talent acquisition team *must* be "students of the business," embedded and knowledgeable about the organization's goals and needs. Human resources must function and be seen as a strategic asset and partner at all levels, as HR is what feeds talent into your traditional revenue-generating business functions.
- In talent acquisition, prioritize quality first and always. Resist the temptation to get butts in seats.
- Fear-based hiring will hold back your organization. The only way for a company to perform at the highest level is to hire based on candidates' potential.
- Never, ever settle for mediocrity.

Combat Control School students assigned to the 352nd Battlefield Airmen Training Squadron are ambushed at their drop-off point during a tactics field training exercise (FTX) at Camp Mackall, North Carolina. The FTX is a culmination of tactics learned in the first year of the Combat Controller (CCT) pipeline, which entails weapons handling, team leader procedures, patrol base operations, troop leading, and small unit tactics under fire in one mission.

*Source: Defense Visual Information Distribution Service / Senior Airman Ryan Conroy*

# CHAPTER 3

# WHAT MAKES SPECIAL OPERATIONS SO SPECIAL?

From the use of the Green Berets during the initial invasion of Afghanistan to the rescue of Captain Phillips to the raids on Al-Qaeda leader Osama bin Laden and ISIS leader Abu Bakr al-Baghdadi—US Special Operations Forces have proven their effectiveness again and again.

People have long been fascinated by the discipline, drive, and determination of these operators, who routinely deliver results, no matter what challenges they face. The business world, in particular, has been drawn to Special Operations because Special Operations Forces are exactly what every business strives to be: innovative, agile, and effective.

Where many businesses get it wrong, Special Operations gets it *right*, leading business leaders to search for the answer to the all-important question: *what makes Special Operations so special?*

In truth, the secret to Special Operations' success is no secret at all. The answer is as simple as the question: *it's the people*. Special Operations Forces succeed because they are composed of talented, high-potential individuals—people like Jonny Kim.

When Jonny Kim entered the Navy, he was a quiet kid, a first-generation Korean American from the Los Angeles area. At first glance, he might be mistaken for any average teenager, but he quickly proved himself to be anything but average. Shortly after high school graduation, Jonny Kim enlisted in the Navy to try out for one of the most elite fighting forces in the world: the Navy SEALS.

In June 2003, at 4:45 a.m. on the first day of BUD/S, Jonny stepped onto the famed quarterdeck, where SEAL candidates undergo hours upon hours of physical training during selection and assessment. Approximately 250 of the nation's best and brightest—from Ivy League graduates to NCAA athletes to former investment bankers—all stood in a line, eager to prove that they had what it takes to be a SEAL. For the simple honor of standing on that beach, each student had completed a rigorous preparatory physical training course. They'd shown the initial aptitude, and now the real assessment and selection were about to begin.

Each year at BUD/S, the cadre of a dozen instructors starts the course by hosing the students down. An instructor then leads the students through a hellacious hour of calisthenics, occasionally sending the students on a sprint to the surf zone 150 meters away. A hundred flutter kicks. Push-ups for two minutes straight. Ten pull-ups. Sprint to the surf and back. Repeat. Wet and sandy, dripping in sweat, the students already feel the pressure from the first minute on. Repeat. Repeat. Repeat. And that concluded the first morning of training.

Over the next six months, the instructors push the students to their mental and physical limits, searching for those who have the drive, mental toughness, and resiliency to make it through to the end. During the infamous Hell Week, the students undergo five days and five nights of professionally led, scientifically orchestrated stress, with no more than two to three hours of sleep total. As the students are sent through one grueling physical activity after another, more and more students walk up and ring the all-too-iconic bell indicating a DOR ("drop on request") to quit BUD/S. By the end of Hell Week, of the 250 candidates who start the school, only thirty to forty will remain, with some classes seeing as few as ten finish the training.

Jonny was one of the few with enough drive, tenacity, and resiliency to make it through BUD/S and become a SEAL. Jonny and Mike completed BUD/S together and went on to serve together at SEAL Team 3 during the Battle of Ramadi (2006) and the Battle of Sadr City (2008). On his first combat deployment, while operating alongside Iraqi soldiers inside the enemy-held city of Ramadi, Jonny heroically ran into the street to pull a wounded Iraqi to safety and rendered medical aid to the soldier. He was awarded the Silver Star for his gallantry. During his second deployment, the Battle for Sadr City, he received the Navy and Marine Corps Commendation Medal with Valor.

Shortly after his second deployment, Jonny was selected for a Navy officer candidate program and attended the University of San Diego, graduating with a 3.98 GPA in mathematics. He then opted to join the Navy Medical Corps, earning a Doctor of Medicine from

Harvard Medical School. Years later, he applied to be an astronaut with NASA. Out of more than eighteen thousand applicants, he was one of twelve chosen to join NASA Astronaut Group 22.

By the age of thirty-four, Jonny Kim had become a combat-decorated Navy SEAL, doctor, and astronaut. Jonny is an incredible human being, but among SEALS, he is not an anomaly.

Soldiers, in general, are already a unique breed, but Special Operations soldiers are their own species. Special Operations Forces (SOF) willingly take on the work that no one else can do, partly out of a sense of duty and partly because they love a great challenge. Time after time, they face the seemingly impossible and win anyway. They consistently push themselves past physical and mental limitations, overcoming all odds to accomplish the mission. They simply refuse to quit. Quitting is not part of their DNA.

When it comes to winning, no one does it better or more consistently than US Special Operations. Their success comes down to their people and a widely held belief:

*Talent + Leadership = Victory*

Special Operations Forces recognize that people are the most critical determinant of success, and as such, they have poured time, energy, and resources into cultivating and honing their assessment and selection of talent. There is no process equal to Special Operations assessment and selection. A deeper look at SOF talent acquisition practices can help your organization better select and develop talent that will achieve greatness. It starts by understanding the fundamental talent mindset that drives Special Operations.

# THE ORIGINS OF THE SOF TALENT MINDSET

While Special Operations Forces can trace their lineage back to the early days of warfare, it was the purpose-formed Special Operations units during World War II—like the Scouts and Raiders (the precursor to SOF units like MARSOC and the Rangers), the First Special Service Force (a joint Canadian-US force), the Underwater Demolition Teams (the precursor to the Navy SEALS), and the Jedburgh teams of the Office of Strategic Services (the precursor to the CIA and Army Special Forces)—that served as the proof of concept, as well as showing the need for a steady-state Special Operations capability in the United States.

In 1962, President John F. Kennedy spearheaded the efforts to increase the capability of the United States military and its ability to wage unconventional and counterinsurgency warfare. President Kennedy could not have been more visionary in responding to the changing nature of war and adapting to the future challenges the United States would face. Technology was evolving rapidly, and the military recognized that old tactics—like large-scale human-wave assaults and trench warfare—were becoming obsolete in the face of smaller counterinsurgency fights. The response was the US Army Special Forces and Special Operations: an innovative arm of the military founded on small teams who could engage in unconventional tactics.

The very core of SOF is a talent mindset: the idea that a small group of talented individuals can be an effective fighting force capable of defeating larger enemy forces and delivering strategic impacts through small-scale operations.

Three innate traits have led to Special Operations' talent mind-set and subsequent success:

1. No one has prior Special Operations experience, so raw talent must be the selection criterion. *The most effective selection is based on mindset and character.*
2. Special Operations Forces are teams. *Teams win, not individuals.*
3. Special Operations teams work in high-stakes environments. *When the stakes are high, mediocrity is unacceptable.*

Let's look more closely at each of these traits.

## NO EMPHASIS ON EXPERIENCE

Raw talent is difficult to identify. Industry experience, on the other hand, is far easier to identify and measure. This is why the business world often falls into a bad habit of overly relying on industry experience as a hiring criterion.

Special Operations does not have that luxury because nobody has prior Special Operations experience. If the sof community began selecting for industry experience, the us would not have a Special Operations community. Out of necessity, Special Operations had to develop a core competency in potential-based hiring, where raw talent is the primary consideration.

## TEAM MENTALITY

Special Operations Forces are structured as teams. They are incentivized as teams, and they win or lose as teams, not individuals.

In contrast, in the business world, egos can often rule, and the team can be less emphasized. People are rewarded for individual achievements, so individuals are often concerned only about their incentives versus the overall health of the organization. Bad leaders who hire and manage others often accept—and even encourage—mediocre employees, because it raises their own value in comparison.

A team mentality greatly reduces the power of ego. It requires that individuals prioritize the team—and thus talent—over oneself. When the person to your right or left has a direct impact on your success, you do not tolerate mediocrity. A single member could bring the entire team down, so it is imperative that Special Operations hold a high standard for talent.

The business world should not be any different. The ultimate incentives are team-based, not individual-based. This changes the entire culture of an organization, leading to the realization that when the organization does better, each individual will naturally do better too.

## HIGH STAKES

Perhaps more than any other factor, the high stakes under which SOF operates necessitate a talent mindset. War and combat are among the most unforgiving environments in the world. A mistake on the battlefield can mean the difference between life and death not only for oneself but for one's fellow soldiers. A failed mission can mean the destruction of cities and the loss of civilian life. Excellence in execution is the standard because it has to be. The stakes are that high. And it should be no different in business.

In business, the risk may not be life-or-death, but the stakes are still incredibly high. Don't fool yourself: business *is* war—war by nonviolent means. The result of a bad hire—or several bad hires—is the underperformance of the business, if not a nosedive to bankruptcy. It is not literal death, but it *is* death in the marketplace. That death spells disaster for you and for your employees, whose well-being depends on the health of your organization.

## ADOPTING THE SOF TALENT MINDSET IN BUSINESS

By design—because of the nonexistent prior experience, the team mentality, and the high stakes—Special Operations Forces must prioritize mindset and character above all else. That's why they've put such an emphasis on assessment, selection, training, and continual evolution of their screening process. In contrast, very few companies have been forced to adopt a talent mindset on the same level.

Special Operations Forces were a necessary response to the changing nature of war. Similarly, businesses need to adapt due to the changing nature of work. And the battlegrounds of business are always changing. Work is becoming increasingly people-driven, which means building and developing a rich talent pool is more important than ever. Accordingly, businesses need to revise and enhance their methods of assessment and selection. This starts by adopting SOF's talent mindset. You can begin doing so by replicating the three factors that lead to the talent mindset: emphasis on attributes and character over industry experience, a team mentality, and high stakes.

In the business world, experience plays a role. We are not suggesting that you disregard experience entirely. However, *industry* experience is not the most reliable indicator of talent. If you want to create a talent mindset, you must place less emphasis on industry experience and more emphasis on talent and character. Don't get us wrong—if you find a candidate with both the requisite experience and character, then hire them immediately. But if you have to choose between experience *or* character, choose character. We will unpack this idea in the next chapter, "Hire for Character; Train for Skill."

Too many people today are self-centered and laser-focused only on trying to further their own careers. They're not working together as an organization or team, naturally inhibiting the true potential of their companies. Fostering a talent mindset requires the buy-in of your employees at all levels of the organization, especially the A-players. In the context of talent acquisition, the best thing you can do is to bring your A-players into the hiring process. When the people in charge of assessment and selection are the same people who will be working on a team with the candidate, there is greater motivation to hire for talent. This concept is covered in depth in chapter 8, "Build Your Hiring Team."

Finally, you must raise the stakes. Many companies accept mediocrity because they don't see it as a real threat, unlike in SOF, where a poor hire can result in death on the battlefield.

Trust us when we say that business is as important as war. The most powerful force in America is not the US military. It's the economy. Your business may be just one small piece of the economy, but each SEAL team, Army Special Forces group, and Ranger battalion is also just one small piece within the US military. Every piece matters. On a macro level, your business is contributing to the United States' most powerful asset; on a micro level, your employees depend upon your company too. Their paychecks, which provide their food and shelter, are directly connected to the success of your business. The stakes are higher than you think.

You must reframe your mindset. The stakes *are* incredibly high, and you must begin taking talent as seriously as Special Operations does. To that end, you should begin acting in accordance with the five Special Operations Forces' truths, which form the foundation of their talent mindset.

## SPECIAL OPERATIONS FORCES' TRUTHS

The five fundamental Special Operations Forces' truths guide everything SOF believes and does, from day-to-day activities to long-term strategic planning. These axioms are at the core of what helps make Special Operations so special, and they directly translate to business truths. If you want to win, in war or business, this is where you start.

| Special Operations Forces' Truths | Business Truths |
| --- | --- |
| Humans are more important than hardware. | Human capital is your most critical resource, your only true competitive advantage in any industry. |
| Quality is better than quantity. | It's not about a head count; it's about talent. |
| Special Operations Forces cannot be mass-produced. | Hard skills can be taught and thus mass-produced, but talent cannot. Talent is innate and hard to create where it does not exist. |
| Competent Special Operations Forces cannot be created after emergencies occur. | Successful talent acquisition requires well-thought-out, forward-thinking planning. It takes time to develop a world-class talent pool. |
| Most Special Operations Forces require non-SOF assistance. | It's a team effort. All supporting business functions, all departments, are crucial to your business's success. |

## 1. HUMANS ARE MORE IMPORTANT THAN HARDWARE

Special Operations Forces are outfitted with the latest technology and equipment—top-of-the-line GPS devices, thermal-imaging goggles, lightweight ballistic armor, underwater rebreathers, and integrated situational awareness systems they can wear on their chest during combat operations. While this hardware certainly offers a competitive advantage, it is nothing compared to the advantage of the humans behind it.

"Technology is just an enhancer," says General William Boykin. "We win with people, end of story."

We would rather have an Army Green Beret armed with a hatchet, "no-quit" attitude, and mission-oriented mindset than any average Joe with the latest high power rifle. Similarly, in the business world, we would rather run a company with great people and limited resources than give mediocre people top-of-the-line machinery.

Hardware (and software too) is only a competitive advantage until your competitors acquire or reach the same capability. In this context, your company's product or service is part of your hardware and cannot offer a long-term competitive advantage. For instance, taxi companies relied on their service as their competitive advantage and grew complacent, never innovating to enhance their service. Meanwhile, talented individuals in ride-sharing startups like Uber and Lyft were innovating, striving to outthink and disrupt the competition, much like SOF is always pushing forward and evolving to create an advantage. Because of their talented people, those ride-sharing companies were able to create a competing service that eliminated taxis' advantage.

Human capital, not your product or service, is your most critical resource, your only true competitive advantage. Human capital is the foundation. Everything else builds on top of it.

## 2. QUALITY IS BETTER THAN QUANTITY

In the early days of the Iraq War, a small task force of operators from a highly selective and specialized Special Operations unit was part of an initial infiltration into western Iraq prior to the main invasion. These specially trained soldiers effectively seized

strategic targets, marked targets for coalition air strikes, and conducted numerous deception operations to confuse the Iraqis as to
the disposition of coalition forces in the west. The small task force
tied up enemy forces that could otherwise have been sent to reinforce against the combined US Army and Marine advance from the
south, effectively deceiving the Iraqis as to where the main effort
would be concentrated. This is the impact a smaller, more capable
and qualified organization can bring to bear on a larger, less capable organization.

Quality is better than quantity. As Colonel Charlie Beckwith,
founder of a highly selective and specialized Army Special
Operations unit, said, *"I'd rather go down the river with seven studs
than with a hundred shitheads."*

History is filled with the stories of smaller, talented teams
defeating far larger forces, in both war and business. Our society
has become enamored with volume, like the obsession with social
media followers, but the pursuit of volume often leads to a reduc-
tion of your standards. Quality will almost always win over quantity. Ten talented salespeople can outsell an untalented team of
fifty or even more.

The business corollary of this truth is that hiring should be
about talent, not head count. This calls back to the butts-in-seat
mentality we introduced in the previous chapter. If you have ten
positions that need to be filled, rather than filling all ten seats with
whoever you can find, it is better to fill five positions with talented
individuals and keep looking. If you're measuring for volume, you
need to stop and begin measuring for quality instead.

## 3. SPECIAL OPERATIONS FORCES CANNOT BE MASS-PRODUCED

At the height of the Global War on Terrorism, the nation's civilian and conventional military leadership requested a sizable increase to our Special Operations Forces. The Army Special Operations community, along with their Air Force, Marine Corps, and Navy counterparts, was essentially told, "We need to make more Special Operations soldiers. Either you guys fix it, or we're going to fix it for you."

SOF did not want to risk their standards being lowered, so they got serious about fixing the problem. The first solution they attempted was to send more people through their pipelines. Theoretically, as long as you put more students into the course, you should end up with more Special Operations soldiers. That is not what happened. Instead, the attrition rate climbed even higher.

BUD/S, like the Army's Special Forces Qualification Course, is not just a training course; it is an *assessment*, *selection*, and training course. BUD/S does not *produce* SEALs; it *reveals* them. Special Operations hires for what they can't teach, and the key traits of talent—drive, resiliency, adaptability, humility, integrity, effective intelligence, team-ability, curiosity, and emotional strength—cannot be taught. Either someone has those attributes, or they don't. This is why Special Operations Forces cannot be mass-produced, even through intensive training programs like BUD/S or the Special Forces Qualification Course (known as Q Course). You can put someone through every single course—Special Operations Combat Medic Course, Breacher Course, Sniper Course, you name it—but if they don't have the fundamental mindset needed to be an operator, they will fail in high-pressure situations.

The same is true in the business world. While you can mass-acquire butts in seats, you cannot mass-acquire talent. "You can't just clone great people and bring them into your organization," says CHRO Tom Lokar. Talent is rare and cannot be manufactured. You cannot take an individual without drive, resiliency, adaptability, humility, integrity, effective intelligence, team-ability, curiosity, and emotional strength and train them into a talented individual. No matter how good the instructors are, no matter how good the training is, you cannot create talent where it does not already exist.

## 4. COMPETENT SPECIAL OPERATIONS FORCES CANNOT BE CREATED AFTER EMERGENCIES OCCUR

On August 6, 2011, Extortion 17, a CH-47D Chinook military helicopter, was shot down by the Taliban during combat operations. It was the largest single loss of life in the Afghan War. Thirty-eight people died, thirty-one of them American. Among the American losses were seventeen Navy SEALs, two Air Force Pararescuemen (PJS), one Air Force Combat Controller (CCT), two Navy Explosive Ordnance Disposal (EOD), two Naval Special Warfare Support Personnel, five Army Aviation personnel, and one military working dog. Most of the Navy SEALs, EOD personnel, and Air Force Special Operators were from a highly selective and specialized SEAL team.

It was an irreparable loss for the families of the fallen and a catastrophic blow to the capability and capacity of our nation.

The highly selective and specialized SEAL team was hit especially hard by the loss, both emotionally and organizationally. If traditional business leaders lost a high percentage of key employ-ees from a single department, they would most likely rush to fill those positions. With a butts-in-seats mentality, standards would be lowered, and the hole caused by the loss of personnel would essentially remain open.

The SEAL community understood, however, that competent Special Operations Forces cannot be created after emergencies occur. Instead of selecting SEALS from other SEAL teams to fill the empty slots, this specialized SEAL team refused to deviate from their time-tested assessment and selection process. The remaining members of the SEAL team stepped up to cover for the absence left by their recently lost brothers-in-arms. In this way, they were able to buy themselves the time needed to rebuild with talent, not bod-ies. Despite the loss from Extortion 17, the SEAL team continues to conduct high-risk missions with a high degree of success to this day, though the loss of life will never be forgotten.

One of the most critical emergencies SOF faces is declaration of war. Every time a war starts, like clockwork, the president and secretary of defense want more Special Operations soldiers, and the SOF leaders always refuse to deviate from the process. When an emergency like war occurs, *time* is limited. You cannot build talent into an organization under time pressure. It takes a long time to turn a high potential into a high performer. The selection of talent is only part one; the development of that talent into a high per-former is part two.

Successful talent acquisition requires well-thought-out, for-ward-thinking planning. It is an eternal pursuit, not something you can turn on and off whenever an emergency occurs. Talent acquisition must be proactive. As CHRO Don Robertson says, "Your hiring can't be reactive. Reactive hiring leads to bad behavior."

One of the most common business corollaries to a wartime emergency is rapid growth. Businesses must stay well ahead of potential growth to establish a viable talent pool to fill critical positions. Otherwise, they will not be able to maintain the level of quality that led to their rapid growth in the first place.

Emergencies require fast, decisive action. If your competitor releases an innovative new product or service that jeopardizes your sales, you don't have time to waste searching for the right people to develop your own product or service in response. You need talent to already be in place when the emergency occurs. The specialized SEAL team was able to continue operating after the Extortion 17 tragedy because they had a small group of talented leaders to step up and lead the organization through the emergency.

## 5. MOST SPECIAL OPERATIONS FORCES REQUIRE NON-SOF ASSISTANCE

Special Operations Forces are supported by an incredible number of people. There are people who gather and analyze intel to guide missions. There are people who handle logistics, like moving equipment from Fort Bragg, North Carolina, to Iraq and coordinating the stocking of everything from beans to bullets to Band-Aids. There are people who handle administrative tasks, making sure that SOF soldiers and all support personnel receive pay and benefits on time so they can focus on the mission at hand.

Special Operations Forces are incredibly respectful and appreciative of their non-SOF support, because they understand that they would not be able to succeed without this support. In the early days of SOF, operators were asked to do everything—logistics, intelligence, and administration. It was an ineffective approach. Operators excel within a certain bandwidth, and they need non-SOF assistance so that they can focus on their strengths and primary mission—winning our nation's battles.

Non-SOF support members are heavily screened, not just for security reasons, but also to identify talent. Non-SOF support is critical to the success of the Special Operators, so they, too, must possess the attributes of talent.

In your company, you likely put a priority on certain departments. For most companies, it might be sales, marketing, engineers, or coders. It is okay to prioritize these roles, but you need talent in every function across your organization. Talent is an organization-wide requirement. To think otherwise can spell doom for your organization.

Company results don't occur in a vacuum. Everything is part of a larger team, so you need talent in all departments and at all levels.

When it comes to talent acquisition and development, few do it better than Special Operations, but even SOF is not perfect at it, not even close. Part of what makes Special Operations so special is that the SOF community recognizes the need for constant improvement.

## ALWAYS EVOLVING

*There is no perfect assessment and selection program.* The best assessment and selection process is the one that is always evolving based on continuous feedback loops.

Don't ever fool yourself into believing a perfect hiring process exists. It doesn't. Even with SOF's highly selective process, there is a bell curve among operators, and someone occasionally becomes an operator who shouldn't have. Green Berets and SEALs, much like bad employees in the private sector, have committed ethics violations, shared sensitive information, and otherwise failed to live up to the standards of the community. The Special Operations community calls these "selection errors."

Whenever a selection error occurs, the Special Operations community takes a brutally hard look at what happened in assessment to allow such an individual into their ranks. As an example, humility was not originally a key trait that SEAL instructors necessarily screened for. After a few SEALs compromised the capability of the community for the sake of elevating their own fame, the community reassessed and determined that humility needed to be a major factor in all selection decisions.

SOF instructors take it very personally when selection errors occur during their tenure. As such, they are proactive, not just reactive, in improving their processes. They investigate all failures of assessment and selection, but they don't wait for a tragedy or a catastrophic mistake. They are always looking for ways to evolve.

Even during SOF assessment and selection courses, the instructors are always evaluating the efficacy of the assessment. Sometimes a student with high potential will drop out of training. In BUD/S, a student might make it through Hell Week and show the drive and resiliency needed to be a SEAL, but something goes wrong, and he rings the DOR bell. The instructors then look at the process and try to determine why he dropped and what they could have done differently to prevent it.

Special Operations selection processes can be constantly refined thanks to *continuous feedback loops*. Following assessment and selection programs, the performance of each graduate is tracked and often cycled back to the cadre of instructors for review. They assess where they went right and, in the rare instance, where they went wrong, and they adjust accordingly.

Effective feedback loops are missing in traditional HR departments. Instead of measuring the *quality* of new hires, companies track how quickly and efficiently hires are made. The only useful feedback that comes back to HR is attrition, and oftentimes that data isn't taken to hiring managers and talent acquisition teams for review and discussion. Without a feedback loop, there is no way to assess the success of the hiring strategies. As such, corporate HR is traditionally not a learning organization. "If you don't look back to judge the efficacies of your thoughts, process, and your systems," asks Brian Decker, "then do you really ever grow?"

It is important for your hiring process to continually evolve. "You have to reinvent the HR function," says CHRO Tracy Keogh. "Things you were doing five years ago probably aren't relevant today or need to be updated. At Hewlett-Packard, we rearticulate our HR strategy every couple of years, and we also are continuously reinventing all of our key processes to make sure that they're still the most relevant for the business and having the kind of impact that we want."

From the inception of Special Operations to now, the prototype of what they're looking for in a candidate has evolved in response to the ever-changing battlefield. In the past, Special Operations soldiers were primarily hardened fighters given the conflicts they fought; today, they must be warrior diplomats. You would be just as likely to see a MARSOC Raider in the State Department building in Pakistan as on the battlefield. Because of the shifting role, the job requirements have changed as well, with candidates being not just more physically fit but also more highly educated and capable.

The exact procedures for assessing and selecting talent have evolved in correlation with the changing role. SOF assessment and selection processes were not built overnight, and they are still being refined. "Each iteration, we're moving closer to what we think is a better solution," says Brian.

How SOF selects its members has been a long learning process of failure and constant innovation and adaptation. In part 2, "Preparing for War," we will share how you can create the foundation for a successful talent acquisition program by applying the many lessons SOF has learned. This begins with reframing your approach to talent acquisition by adopting a strategy of hiring for talent and training for skill.

## KEY TAKEAWAYS

- By necessity, Special Operations Forces have adopted a deep talent mindset. SOF's team mentality and the high stakes of war reinforce the importance of talent, and because it's impossible for candidates to have prior SOF experience, the SOF community has been forced to find better ways to identify talent.

- Five truths drive everything Special Operations Forces do, and these truths apply to business as much as the military:
  1. Humans are more important than hardware.
  2. Quality is better than quantity.
  3. Special Operations Forces cannot be mass-produced.
  4. Competent Special Operations Forces cannot be created after emergencies occur.
  5. Most Special Operations Forces require non-SOF assistance.
- SOF assessment and selection processes are so effective because they are constantly evolving, thanks to robust feedback loops.

# PART II

# PREPARING FOR WAR

Marines perform pull-ups during Phase I of the US Marine Corps Forces Special Operations Command's assessment and selection course aboard Marine Corps Base Camp Lejeune, North Carolina. Completing a physical fitness test with a minimum score of 225 is one of many physical, mental, and intellectual prerequisites to become a Critical Skills Operator with MARSOC or Special Operations.

*Source: Defense Visual Information Distribution Service / Lance Cpl. Steven Fox*

# CHAPTER 4

# HIRE FOR CHARACTER; TRAIN FOR SKILL

eter Schutz, former CEO of Porsche, said, "Hire character. Train skill."

This strategy is more important today than ever, yet for many business leaders and hiring managers, it has become meaningless. *"Hire for character; train for skill" is clinically dead in today's business environment.* There's one simple reason why: hiring for skill is objective and easy. You can count the number of years of experience someone has or quantify how many languages a software engineer can use well. Hiring for character, on the other hand, is subjective and more difficult. Most people take the easy route. That is human nature. So hiring for character is a skill only a few astute and dedicated hiring managers or business leaders ever develop.

Let us tell you about a scenario that we have seen all too often, where Daniel, the hiring manager for a midsize manufacturing company, made the mistake of hiring for experience instead of character.

Daniel was looking to hire a candidate for a sales leadership position, and he used two search firms—EF Overwatch (our recruiting firm) and a competitor.

*Jeremy—presented by a competitive search firm*
- 3.9 GPA from a prestigious university—high intelligence
- Four years of industry experience with two different companies
- Driven, highly competent, but borderline arrogant

*Chris—presented by EF Overwatch*
- 3.2 GPA from a public university—above-average intelligence
- Faced significant adversity in life (came from a lower-middle-class family and held a full-time job while in college)
- Recently separated Army infantry officer who held several different functional billets in the Army
- Has all the attributes required to be a highly successful sales leader but lacks industry experience

Which of these candidates would you choose? Since this chapter is about hiring for character and training for skill, you might know that the answer is most likely Chris, not Jeremy. But be honest: at your company, which one of these candidates would most likely be hired?

Most companies would choose Jeremy without hesitation. Chris's GPA was average compared to Jeremy's, and he didn't have industry-specific experience, but he was one of those people who performed time and time again. Whatever you put in front of him, he would find a way through it, over it, or around it. He was relentless and adaptable.

Despite Chris's strengths, he'd been passed over by many companies. Most never even called him in for an interview, sending his application straight to the resume black hole because of his lack of industry experience. When he did make it to the interview phase, everybody loved him. He was articulate and had a great attitude. No one doubted his ability, but they saw him as a risk because he didn't have the experience or an already built list of industry contacts.

Daniel ultimately chose Jeremy over Chris. Two weeks later, he called Mike and George and told them, "We made a huge mistake." He explained that Jeremy had no humility and was not receptive to direction. None of the people working with him—not his leaders, peers, or team members—felt he was a team player. Jeremy was what is known as "high performance, low trust" in the Special Operations community.

Chris had the character, and Jeremy had the skills. With Chris's learning ability, he would have been able to pick up the needed technical skills for the role within a matter of months, if not weeks. In contrast, it would be nearly impossible to teach Jeremy the needed team-ability and humility, even with years of work.

Daniel and his team didn't want to fire Jeremy because it would look like a bad hire (which it was) and draw unwanted attention from their senior leaders. So Jeremy stayed in his role for a year. In that time, attrition among his team skyrocketed, and sales went down. He brought far more damage than value. His department was unrecognizable as what it had been, both in terms of the team and the culture. The company finally fired Jeremy, but it's unclear how long it will take for them to fully recover from that bad hire.

Meanwhile, Chris was offered a position as a senior consultant at a management consulting firm. In less than a year, he became a successful project manager, building out his own team and driving exceptional results.

Daniel had made a very costly mistake. But it was a mistake he would learn from. Factoring in the costs of hiring, onboarding, and exiting Jeremy, Daniel's company had wasted thousands of dollars, to say nothing of the lost opportunity cost associated with *not* hiring Chris as well as the immeasurable cost of the toxic culture Jeremy created. By the time Daniel finally replaced Jeremy, the company had spent an entire year without needed leadership in a key department. That meant twelve months operating below their full potential—twelve months of lowered output, twelve months of reduced revenue, twelve months behind their competition.

Daniel's mistake was the same one that countless companies make every day: he'd hired based on a resume, hiring for industry experience, not character. Character is infinitely more important in hiring decisions than skill or industry experience because while you can train skill, you can't train character. That bears repeating: *you can train skill, but you can't train character.* If you only change one thing about your talent acquisition process, it should be hiring for character and training for skill. Stop hiring based on resumes. Stop hiring based on university degrees. Stop hiring based on industry experience. Instead, start hiring character. Start hiring *talent.*

## HIRE FOR WHAT YOU CAN'T TEACH

Herb Kelleher, iconic business leader and co-founder of Southwest Airlines, once said,

> We draft great attitudes. If you don't have a good attitude, we don't want you, no matter how skilled you are. We can change skill levels through training. We can't change attitude.[9]

Kelleher's approach makes logical sense: hire for what you can't teach. Yet today, many companies do the exact opposite, hiring based on skills and industry experience. Imagine if the Special Operations community hired based on industry experience. *We would have literally zero Special Operations soldiers in our ranks.* The only people with prior SOF experience would be SOF soldiers from foreign countries, and we don't think we need to explain why that would be a terrible idea. Despite—arguably, *because* of—the fact that they can't hire based on experience, the Special Operations community has become a world-class organization and a model for efficiency, effectiveness, innovation, and agility.

Nobody comes into Special Operations already possessing the needed skills. Marine Corps Special Operations Command (MARSOC) Raiders, for example, must be able to safely handle and employ demolitions. They must be able to safely and accurately

---

9    Elisabeth Brier, "Herb Kelleher, Legendary Southwest Founder: From the Forbes Archives," *Forbes*, January 4, 2019, https://www.forbes.com/sites/elisabethbrier/2019/01/04/herb-kelleher-legendary-southwest-founder-from-the-forbes-archives.

shoot their weapons systems. They must be able to skydive out of planes. No candidate enters MARSOC already possessing all those skills, and they don't need to, because part of MARSOC is teaching those skills. Even after the successful completion of an assessment and selection phase, new Special Operations soldiers are not thrown into the arena of combat without first undergoing unit-level training to prepare for war. During that unit-level training, young operators are constantly mentored and coached by senior Special Operations soldiers.

When retired Navy SEAL Commander Rich Diviney became involved in the selection and assessment for a highly selective and specialized SEAL unit, he quickly discovered that they needed to stop looking at skills and instead look at character attributes. "We can always teach a guy how to shoot and hit a target or how to jump out of an airplane. Those are skills," he explained. "What we can't necessarily teach is the ability to run into a room, decide in a moment's notice who to shoot and who not to shoot, and do so in a safe way and then continue moving. For that, you need the right character attributes, like situational awareness [or effective intelligence] and adaptability."

Remember the second SOF truth: Special Operations Forces cannot be mass-produced. Talent cannot be taught. While you can teach someone how to safely skydive, you cannot teach someone the drive and resiliency needed to succeed in Special Operations or any industry, for that matter.

Business leaders often tell us that they need hires with previous industry experience and technical skills in order for their company to compete. That's simply untrue. You can teach a candidate the needed hard skills, and you can give them industry experience. You can't teach those raw ingredients of talent. As Don says, "I look for three primary things when selecting someone. I look for *raw intelligence* because I can't make you smart. I look for *energy* because I can't give you energy. I look for *positive mentality* because I can't give you a positive outlook."

The most successful talent acquisition programs are founded on the strategy of hiring for what you can't teach. That means hiring for character—those aspects of a person that are impossible (or incredibly difficult and time-consuming) to teach.

Many organizations agree with this concept in theory, but in practice, they rely on hard skills, industry experience, and resumes to make their hiring decisions. These three methods of candidate assessment do play a role in talent acquisition, but it is a much smaller role than you might expect.

---

### PERSONALITY ≠ CHARACTER

Personality and character are not the same thing. Character is a person's deep inner attributes that drive their decisions and behaviors. Personality is how someone outwardly presents themselves to the world. Drive, resiliency, adaptability, humility, integrity, effective intelligence, team-ability, curiosity, and emotional strength are all character traits. Personality is how someone exhibits those traits externally: they may be loud or quiet, obnoxious or charming.

---

Personality frequently determines a person's likability, and likability is one of the top criteria people use in hiring, especially in interviews. In general, we are biased toward hiring who we like—the people we'd want to get a beer with. This is a horrible way to hire for many reasons. First, people can trick you into liking them, especially in a limited interaction like a hiring process. Second, hiring the people you like is a recipe for creating a workplace where everyone looks and acts exactly the same. That leads to groupthink.

SOF operators have become seasoned at identifying the difference between likability and the ability to perform. It's not uncommon to hear a SOF operator describe another operator as the type of guy you would love to have a beer with but would never step onto the battlefield with.

Ultimately, what matters is whether a person can perform in the role, not how likable they are.

There is one important caveat: while you don't need to like someone, you do need to be able to work with them. Mike and his fellow SEALs weren't necessarily all friends, but they were all brothers, and they were able to come together as a team to accomplish the mission.

Try to eliminate your bias for likability. Hire for character, not personality.

## HARD SKILLS ARE TEACHABLE

Hard skills are the specific, easier-to-teach skills required to execute the fundamental functions of a job. Examples of hard skills range from typing and Microsoft Office skills to accounting, marketing, or computer programming.

In the hierarchy of what you look for in talent, these skills fall near the bottom, because they can be taught or gained through experience. Hard skills tend to be less important than companies believe, especially for management roles. In fact, when Google did an employee survey to identify the traits of its most successful managers, technical abilities ranked dead last.[10]

Now, obviously, you wouldn't hire someone for a programming job if they don't know how to program. For every position, there is a minimum standard that everyone has to meet for hard skills. The trick is that after someone meets the minimum standard, you stop looking at hard skills and instead look for those all-important, difficult-to-teach character attributes.

As an example, the 2020 minimum required number of pull-ups for Green Berets is six. Anyone who wants to be a Green Beret *must* do a minimum of six pull-ups. But doing more than six pull-ups does not give you an advantage. (That said, Green Beret candidates all aim for a personal standard well above six pull-ups.) As LTC Brian Decker said of the US Army Special Forces assessment and

---

10 Michael Schneider, "Google Employees Weighed In on What Makes a Highly Effective Manager (Technical Expertise Came in Last)," *Inc.*, June 20, 2017, https://www.inc.com/michael-schneider/google-did-an-internal-study-that-will-forever-change-how-they-hire-and-promote-.html.

selection, "Once you cross a minimum threshold, physical measures are no longer really of any value." Someone can do twenty pull-ups, but if they don't have high drive and resiliency, they won't become a Green Beret. Similarly, someone with the right mindset who does the minimum six pull-ups may become one of the highest-performing Green Berets in their outfit.

There are people in the Special Operations community who hit the bare minimum on all the hard skills in initial training and go on to become amazing operators because of their character. The SOF community isn't looking for marathon runners, bodybuilders, boxing champions, or Olympic swimmers, so after the minimum physical standards are met, there is no reason to continue factoring physical ability into the selection decision. This does not excuse SOF operators from maintaining the highest standard of physical fitness after completing training. Physical fitness level in the military, much like in life, is often a telltale sign of drive, discipline, and high personal standards. Retired Air Force Colonel Dr. Carroll Greene, who has studied the performance of Special Operations soldiers for over twenty-five years and who helped shape the operational psychology applications for USSOCOM, admittedly states, "There is an undeniable correlation between being physically fit and handling stress well, being able to make good judgments under pressure."

Any minimum requirements for hard skills should be true *requirements* to complete the job. As CHRO Tracy Keogh says, "I have to make sure that whatever we're using as screening criteria makes sense and that we're continuously reanalyzing whether it's still relevant." This isn't just a smart idea; it's also a standard the

Equal Employment Opportunity Commission uses to judge a company's hiring process.

A great example of a company failing to do this is when a functional manager asked George to find someone with five years of Python coding experience when Python had only been around for three and a half years. George was quick to correct the hard skills requirements and refocus the manager on identifying a talented hire with high learning ability.

Just like hard skills, companies tend to place too much weight on industry experience.

## INDUSTRY EXPERIENCE IS NOT AS IMPORTANT AS YOU THINK

General William Boykin was at the US Army John F. Kennedy Special Warfare Center and School (SWCS, pronounced "Swick") for the creation of the X-Ray Program, or 18X, in 2000. The school had been drawing all of its candidates from conventional military units, but those units did not want to give up their better soldiers to Special Operations. "They were finding all kinds of reasons to block us," General Boykin said, "and even when we got soldiers, we were having trouble getting them all the way through the school."

Their solution was 18X, which is a program to prepare civilian candidates for direct access into Special Forces (SF) assessment, selection, and training. Through this program, civilian candidates are sent to Fort Benning to attend infantry One Station Unit Training (OSUT), which combines Army Basic Training and Infantry Advanced Individual Training, followed by Airborne ("Jump") School. Following completion of OSUT and Jump School,

18X candidates check into SWCS at Fort Bragg to enter into SF assessment and selection.

"There was a lot of apprehension about the program," General Boykin said. "People were worried we were going to lower the standards." To address those concerns, they actually set a higher standard for 18X candidates in educational, intelligence, and physical levels. For starters, 18X candidates must have a high school degree as well as high scores on the Armed Services Vocational Aptitude Battery (ASVAB), the military aptitude assessment used by every service.

Statistically, 18X candidates have proved to be excellent Special Operations soldiers, despite not having previous military experience. In fact, the lack of military experience is often an advantage. "They're bright. They're motivated. They're educated," General Boykin says. "And you don't have to break bad habits that they developed in other places. Once they leave Fort Benning and they get to Fort Bragg, they're yours. What you do with them from that point on is up to you."

Although the Army's Special Forces 18X candidates were initially looked at with "a lot of suspicion and apprehension," General Boykin said, "maybe 60 percent of the ranks, if not more, are now 18 X-Rays." Army Special Forces is not alone in recruiting directly from civilian applicant pools. The Air Force, Army, Marine, and Navy Special Operations communities today pull the large majority of their candidates from what they call "the street" rather than "the active-duty ranks."

Prior service candidates (those currently serving in the conventional military), despite entering with basic military skills, are not any more likely to succeed in Special Operations assessment and selection than civilian candidates. During Dr. Josh Cotton's time with the SEALS, studies showed that civilian candidates were *more* likely to graduate from BUD/s than those candidates with prior military experience. It may seem counterintuitive at first, but ultimately, what's going to make a SOF operator successful is their mindset, not prior military (industry) experience.

As the Special Operations community has discovered, industry experience is not necessarily predictive of talent. Just because somebody has industry experience does not mean they will be a good performer, and vice versa: just because someone does *not* have industry experience does not mean they won't be a good performer.

As another example, LTC Brian Decker once put a group of MBA students and a group of undergraduate scholarship students through a mini team week designed from the Green Beret assessment and selection process. The MBA students were selected based on GMAT scores and undergraduate experience, while the undergraduates were selected using a "whole-person" process focusing on character. According to Brian, "The undergraduate group ran circles around the MBA group. They weren't afraid to experiment and had the humility to ask, 'What do you think?' whereas the MBAS were so political, they couldn't get stuff done. They literally would do the task in three times the amount of time as the undergraduates." Most would have expected the graduate students to outperform undergrads due to their greater experience, but as Brian discovered, character was more important.

Experience tells you where someone has been, but character tells you where they are going. Brian has spent the past ten years studying "the traits, learning and development processes, and experiences of those who go on to be great in a broad range of domains." He has discovered that if you "remove the domain expertise and look at the [character] traits, they are very similar." We're not advocating that you disregard experience entirely. You're not going to hire a kid straight out of high school for a C-suite position. Experience and past performance matter for certain positions. But you do need to be thoughtful about how you use experience in your selection process. We see companies make three common mistakes when it comes to looking at experience:

1. They require experience that doesn't matter to job performance.
2. They require very specific experience when general experience would be just as good.
3. They prioritize industry experience over character.

Just as you want minimum requirements for hard skills to make sense, you want minimum requirements for experience to make sense. With the 18X program, SOF leaders asked themselves, "Does having infantry experience really matter?" and the answer was no. Special Operations is so unique that being part of the conventional forces is not an indicator of being a good fit for Special Operations. Since the prior experience isn't required to perform the job, it should not be a minimum requirement.

The second mistake is that companies look for incredibly specific industry experience when general experience would be just as valuable. Think back to our opening story for this chapter. Did it really matter that Chris didn't have sales experience within the manufacturing industry? No! What the company really needed for that role was a good *leader*, and Chris did have leadership experience, in fact, much more than Jeremy.

"Everybody wants a specialist," says Brian Decker. "It's not enough to be an ear doctor; I've got to be a left-ear doctor. The problem is that's not how Special Operations soldiers are trained. *We're generalists. We all have some degree of specialty, but it's the ability to work broadly across a wide range of functions that makes us special*...Everyone is a product of their education and life experience. As generalists, we draw upon a vast range of experiences to gain insight into complex problems."

If you want to hire the best talent, look at experience related to their character. Do they have past experience that shows drive or resiliency or adaptability? Have they proven themselves a good leader, or have they shown that they can work as part of a team?

The last but most frequent mistake companies make is prioritizing industry experience over character. When companies hire this way, they are typically looking for somebody to make a lateral move—to perform their same role, simply at their company instead of a competitor's. The majority of the time, if somebody is going to change companies, it is to make more money or move up in their role. If you are encouraging lateral moves, it often forces you into a situation of (1) paying more than your competitors for the same level of talent or (2) hiring non-talent. Sometimes there's a valid reason for a talented individual to move laterally without a pay raise—like an issue of workplace culture or a relocation—but often, if someone is willing to move laterally without a significant pay raise, they are not top talent.

We all have a bias to think our team—our company—is better, but be honest and ask yourself, "Why would this person give up everyone and everything they know to do that same job with only a small pay increase?"

Prior industry experience is simply not the most effective predictor of performance. You likely have average performers within your company who have years of experience, right? What makes you think any other company is different? Sometimes hiring based on experience simply means inheriting bad habits or mediocre performers from a competitor, like Jeremy from the opening story.

Another reason prior experience is a poor predictor of performance is that nobody works in a vacuum. A person's performance at a company is dependent on the environment and the team they operate within. "The world is littered with superstars at one company who fail at another," says Don Robertson. You can see this in sports. A number one draft pick who excelled at his university or with his prior team is drafted to a new team, and he no longer performs as well. Conversely, someone who was previously average could become a rock star after being traded to a new team. Simply put, context matters, and you can't always know the context a candidate is leaving behind.

Finally, if all you are doing is hiring from the same few talent pools, you will not be able to grow your organization in a new direction. Sometimes all it takes is someone approaching a problem from a new perspective to solve the seemingly unsolvable. Brian Decker is a great example of this. He now works in the NFL as the Indianapolis Colts' Director of Player Development. He helps to select draft picks and develop players to their full potential. The fact that he comes from outside the NFL community is one of his greatest strengths, as he questions the status quo and innovates in ways others never thought of. "I wasn't hired because of what I know. I was hired because of what I don't know," he says. "I'm in an industry where everybody's been around for tens of years. I don't have that experience, so I look at everything differently."

Ultimately, yes, you should consider and evaluate a candidate's experience, but don't obsess over it. What they know and where they have been is all in the past. Their character—what makes them who they are, what energizes them, how they respond to stress— will determine their future. Hire for the future, not the past.

## DOES CULTURE FIT MATTER?

"Businesses fall into two classic mistakes," says CHRO Don Robertson. "You'll either look for a skillset, or you'll look for a culture fit, rather than looking for someone who actually has the ingredients to do the role." Many companies place too much emphasis on culture fit, but as Don himself points out, "You can't ignore the culture fit," either.

You have to take the time to define the character of your organization. If you don't get that part right, then you won't know what you're looking for in new hires. Perhaps one company is more collaborative and another individualistic; maybe one is more relaxed and another more hard-driving. However, if you are hiring for adaptability, as we recommend, then your new hires should be able to adapt to your culture.

In determining culture fit, the most important thing to focus on is "Can this person buy in and believe in this organization? Can they see themselves being part of it?" As long as the answers to those questions are yes, then the person is a good fit for your business.

## THE ROLE OF RESUMES

Resumes are great sources of information, but you have to dig to find it. Too many companies use resumes as a superficial screening tool instead of looking deeper. A 2019 ad campaign from Indeed said it best: "You're not hiring a resume; you're hiring a person."

Too often, companies draw conclusions from resumes that seem logical but are inaccurate. For example, hiring based on IQ is a scientifically valid method of hiring for success. But resumes don't include IQ scores, so companies often look at GPA instead. They assume a high GPA means a high IQ and a low GPA means low IQ. It's a reasonable conclusion, but like much of what you see on a resume, what you are inferring is not always reality. What GPA really shows is how good of a *student* someone was, and you're not trying to hire a student. Boston University researcher Eric Barker found that most valedictorians gain only moderate amounts of success, not wild amounts of success, like becoming millionaires. Barker argues that the traits that make successful students—like complying with rules—are not the same traits that make innovators and millionaires.[11] High GPA probably means the person is smart, but a low GPA doesn't mean the person is not smart. See the difference?

Instead of looking at the superficial picture, look at what candidates have actually accomplished. Simply having X number of years of experience is not as strong of a predictor of high performance as actual examples of past high performance. You want to look at how a candidate contributed to the success of the company. It's not about simply doing the job; it's about how *well* someone does the job, helping the organization accomplish the mission.

You also have to look at the story behind the resume. "The big difference between Special Operations and the private sector," says LTC Brian Decker, "is the private sector abdicates their selection process to academic institutions, to credentials and resumes. We don't do that. We look at those types of things, but we're more concerned about the input that goes into accomplishments." He continues, "Stop looking at the resume, other than to see what outcomes this person's achieved, and start trying to understand the process by which they arrived, because that's the part that translates."

The "facts" of the resume—a person's education, the companies they've worked for, the jobs they've held—tell only part of the story. You don't want to know just *what* they've done; you want to know *how* they've done it. In most cases, they won't be doing the exact same thing at your company as at their previous company, so you want to unearth those fundamental character attributes that enabled them to accomplish what they've accomplished. Those are

---

11  Shana Lebowitz, "Why Valedictorians Rarely Become Rich and Famous—and the Average Millionaire's College gpa is 2.9," *Entrepreneur*, May 30, 2017, https://www.entrepreneur.com/article/295095.

the building blocks that predict performance, and they are constant and translate from role to role.

Regina Hartley has a fantastic TED Talk, "Why the Best Hire Might Not Have the Perfect Resume,"[12] about the need to look at the story a resume tells. As she explains it, some people go through life without facing many obstacles. These people—the "silver spoons"—are the ones with the perfect resumes: Ivy League school, 4.0 GPA, good industry experience. On the other end of the spectrum, those who have faced a lot of adversity in their lives—the "scrappers"—often have imperfect resumes: a degree from a state school, a lower GPA, but a history of overcoming obstacle after obstacle.

If you make hiring decisions based on a resume, you will choose more silver spoons than scrappers. Silver spoons can be fantastic employees, but so can scrappers. Scrappers are often the ones with the most resiliency and drive. They've faced obstacles and overcome them. Through adversity, they've built a mission-first, never-quit mentality. They've had to fight and work so hard and so often that accomplishment is like muscle memory for them. Both silver spoons and scrappers can be high performers, but too often, scrappers never even get the chance to interview.

Talent doesn't fit a mold. When you get an imperfect resume that looks different, you need to investigate further. A candidate may have a lower GPA because they had to work through college, or they may have an unusual job history because they had to do whatever it took to make ends meet. That person may have more

---

12 Regina Hartley, "Why the Best Hire Might Not Have the Perfect Resume," TED, September 2015, https://www.ted.com/talks/regina_hartley_why_the_best_hire_might_not_have_the_perfect_resume.

drive, resiliency, adaptability, and humility than the candidates with seemingly perfect resumes. The "perfect" resumes must be investigated too. A high GPA at an Ivy League school could indicate someone with intense drive who is willing to put in the work to excel in a competitive environment. Or it could mean someone who is used to always succeeding. A person with a perfect resume might crumble at the first sign of pressure.

In the next chapter, we'll take a look at the nine attributes of talent—fundamental characteristics you *can't* teach: drive, resiliency, adaptability, humility, integrity, effective intelligence, team-ability, curiosity, and emotional strength.

## KEY TAKEAWAYS

- Hire for what you can't teach and train for what you can. That means hiring for character and training for hard skills.
- Personality is not the same thing as character. You should hire based on the core character traits that predict performance, not based on likability.
- Set appropriate minimum standards for hard skills, but don't obsess over finding applicants that exceed the minimums to the exclusion of character.
- Industry experience is the number one factor companies use in the hiring process, yet it is a poor predictor of success. Look beyond industry experience to patterns of success.
- Resumes tell a story. Look deeper, past the surface-level facts, to understand the candidate's character.

US Army soldiers conduct a ruck march during the Cultural Support Assessment and Selection program. The US Army Special Operations Command's cultural support program prepares all-female soldier teams to serve as enablers supporting Army Special Operations–combat forces in and around secured objective areas. The Cultural Support Assessment and Selection program is conducted by the US Army John F. Kennedy Special Warfare Center and School at Fort Bragg, North Carolina, and is five days of physical, mental, and intellectual evaluations designed to determine a candidate's ability to maintain her composure, apply logic, communicate clearly, and solve problems in demanding environments.

*Source: Defense Visual Information Distribution Service / Staff Sgt. Russell Klika*

# CHAPTER 5

# THE NINE FOUNDATIONAL CHARACTER ATTRIBUTES OF TALENT

Under pressure, at one's mental and physical limits, hard skills rapidly degrade. What remains is *character*. "Skills are, by design, meant for predictable situations and environments," says retired SEAL Commander Rich Diviney. "If businesses are interested in forming organizations and teams that effectively deal with unpredictability and complexity, they have to go deeper than the guy who has the best sales record or the Harvard grad who's at the top of the class. They have to look at character."

Character is key because it is an indicator of a person's capacity. General William Boykin points to capacity as more important than current ability: "What are you looking for—hard skills or capacity? Ideally, you look for both, but if you have to choose, and you have a fair way of doing so, assess their capacity. What is their capacity to learn new skills? What's their capacity to think for themselves? What's their capacity to problem-solve?" According to General Boykin, it is this focus on capacity that has made Special Operations so successful on the battlefield and beyond.

A person's character is the aggregate of their deeply ingrained attributes. As we define it, the nine foundational character attributes of high-potential individuals are:

- Drive
- Resiliency
- Adaptability
- Humility
- Integrity
- Effective intelligence
- Team-ability
- Curiosity
- Emotional strength

These traits are predictors of high performance. These attributes cannot be taught, so they should be the focus of your hiring.

## THE ATTRIBUTES OF AN OPERATOR

The different Special Operations Forces each look for something slightly different in their ideal operator, but there are many similarities and overlaps. Military psychologist Dr. Carroll Greene says, "All the SOF communities are looking for 85 percent of the same variables in the people that they recruit." It's like they're all looking for ice cream, but each has their favorite flavor. Here are the attributes that Army Special Forces, MARSOC, and the Navy SEALS have identified as critical to performance.

### Army Special Forces

- Integrity
- Courage
- Perseverance
- Personal responsibility

- Professionalism
- Adaptability
- Being a team player
- Capability

### MARSOC

- Integrity
- Effective intelligence
- Physical ability
- Adaptability
- Initiative

- Determination
- Dependability
- Teamwork
- Interpersonal skills
- Stress tolerance

### Navy SEALS

- Physical courage
- Moral courage
- Humility

- Creativity
- Team-ability
- Resiliency

## DRIVE

Drive is the need for achievement. An individual with high drive wants to be the best, has a desire to grow and push themselves, is willing to take risks, and often seeks out fresh achievements.

LTC Brian Decker identifies drive as a key trait among Green Berets. "They all have high-end desire. They have a growth mindset and feel they can do anything if they set their minds to it," he says. "Desire is fundamental to success at any level, and you can't coach desire." The difference between a Green Beret who continually delivers results on the battlefield and their counterparts who do not often comes down to their level of drive.

Those with high drive are always looking forward to the next goal and challenge. If someone with low drive makes a million-dollar deal, they might pat themselves on the back for months. For someone with high drive, it will be just hours or days before they start asking, "All right, what's next?"

High-drive individuals are never satisfied. They're continually hungry for achievement. While high drive often correlates with increasingly bigger paychecks, drive is not about money; it's about growth. Those with high drive are driven to find results, not glory. They simply want to be better than they were yesterday. When we asked a SEAL with particularly high drive, "Who are you comparing yourself to?" the SEAL gave us a confused look and said, "Nobody. I just know I can be better."

High drive is a strong indicator of future high performers because those with strong drive are self-motivated and will only continue to improve. Microsoft CEO Satya Nadella calls these people "learn-it-alls," and he argues that you'll get better results by hiring "learn-it-alls" instead of "know-it-alls."

Some may say driven people have a bit of ego that propels them, and we would not debate that. The best SOF operators *do* have a hint of ego, but not at the expense of the entire team or organization's success. As Rich Diviney says, "The individuals who make it through BUD/S [and other Special Operations assessment and selection courses] do so because they want to be the best. That's narcissism to a small degree. You need to have some narcissism, but you can't go past the tipping point." It's about balance—a concept Leif Babin and Jocko Willink wrote about in their book *The Dichotomy of Leadership*. For this reason, it's important that high drive is paired with humility and team-ability.

## RESILIENCY

Someone with high resiliency bounces back from stress quickly, is adaptable, and is not easily discouraged. An individual with high resiliency resists quitting and is focused on completing goals. Essentially, resiliency is how people handle setbacks and persevere in the face of challenges. They accept failure as part of the process. They don't accept it passively but utilize their lessons learned and mistakes as a basis to grow.

Imagine someone *loses* a million-dollar deal. For someone with low resiliency, this failure could derail them, setting them back for months or even for life. Someone with high resiliency would recover more quickly and begin working on securing the next million-dollar deal. Setbacks and failures are inevitable; it's part of the process of life. How people handle those challenges is what truly matters. Someone who can fall down a hundred times and still get back up is exactly the kind of talent you want in your company. Special Operations assessment and selection is intentionally designed to knock people down, again and again, to see how they react to failure.

Special Operations is filled with stories of resiliency. For instance, in 2007, during a direct-action raid in Al Anbar Province, Iraq, to capture a high-level Al-Qaeda leader, Navy SEAL Mike Day entered a room occupied by four terrorists. They immediately opened fire. He killed two before being knocked out by an enemy grenade. He was shot a total of twenty-seven times. Eleven rounds were stopped by his body armor, but the remaining sixteen tore through his body. When he woke up, the remaining two terrorists were firing at the rest of his SEAL platoon outside the building. Despite being severely wounded, he drew his pistol, killed the remaining two terrorists, and somehow managed to walk to the CASEVAC (casualty evacuation) without assistance. Despite being severely wounded and one year away from being eligible to retire, Mike returned to duty four months after being wounded. He took over an advanced training cell for SEALS, committed to continuing to provide value to the SOF community by training the future generation of special operators for the challenges that awaited them. This is just one of thousands of stories exemplifying the high resiliency within the US Special Operations community.

The business world is filled with stories of leaders who, at one point, hit rock bottom and lost everything, only to bounce back and exceed their previous success, like Bernie Marcus and Arthur Blank, the co-founders of Home Depot. In the late 1970s, they were part of the senior management for Handy Dan, a home improve-ment chain. Following an acquisition of Handy Dan's parent com-pany, Marcus and Blank were both fired. It was a crushing blow, but they didn't give up. They struck out on their own, and thus, Home Depot was born.

You can't teach that type of resiliency, but you certainly want it in your company. As CEO Joe DePinto says, "I want to see people step up, fail fast, iterate quickly, and improve."

Resiliency came up time and time again as we talked with mil-itary and business leaders. Brian Decker pointed to resiliency as critical for Green Berets:

> They are resilient—they have tried and failed and see this as part of the development process. All growth happens at the limits of our ability—when our systems adapt to the demands of an increas-ingly difficult requirement. They have learned the value of effort and persistence in the face of adversity. They are comfortable being uncomfortable.

Resiliency is also a measure of how someone handles challenges in the pursuit of a long-term goal. BUD/S is purposefully designed as a series of increasingly difficult barriers to overcome because SEALS must have tenacity. On the battlefield, you don't want the guy with the biggest muscles on your team if he's going to give up at the first sign of challenge; you'd be better off with the scrawny kid who's only 160 pounds but has no quit in him. It doesn't matter what you look like, big or small; what matters is the refusal to quit or accept the status quo. That's what success is—overcoming barrier after barrier.

An important aspect of resiliency is discipline. People with high discipline are process-driven and put in the necessary work each day that will take them closer to their long-term goals. Jocko Willink, retired Navy SEAL and coauthor of *New York Times* bestseller *Extreme Ownership*, has credited his success in life to his unshakable discipline. Jocko wakes up at four thirty every morning and starts his day with physical training before heading to work. Jocko has become a social media icon for a number of reasons, but his daily Instagram posts of his Timex watch at 4:30 a.m. have played a large role in attracting his over 1 million followers. His discipline has inspired hundreds of thousands, and he is now sponsored by Timex. One of Jocko's favorite quotes is "Discipline equals freedom."

BUD/S is perhaps the most physically demanding military training course in the world. But it is resiliency, not physical ability, that predicts a student's success. Many Olympic and NCAA athletes have gone to BUD/S and failed because they are used to always winning and being the best. When they get to BUD/S, many of them can't emotionally handle *not* winning. They don't have resiliency—the mental ability to handle stress, challenges, and failure.

Retired SEAL Master Chief Jason Tuschen, former Command Master Chief of Naval Special Warfare Group ONE and current CEO of Randori Inc., says, "My favorite guy at BUD/S is the kid of average athletic ability who on Monday's run might make it by one second, and on Wednesday's he'll miss it by two seconds. But you know he has given it 110 percent, and that's a much better individual than the NCAA Division I All-American who is coasting through. He's not giving it all...I'd rather have the kid of average athletic ability make it through because I know he's going to always bust his ass and do everything he can in his power to overcome his weaknesses."

People with high resiliency get up each day and say, "I know it's going to be harder today, and that's what I'm here for." These people are more likely to become high performers.

## ADAPTABILITY

Adaptability is the ability to adjust one's behavior and actions according to what the situation requires. If you have somebody with high drive and high resiliency but zero adaptability, they're not going to be one of your best performers. It's that old saying: "The definition of insanity is doing the same thing over and over again and expecting a different result." Adaptability is the difference between insanity and innovation.

Adaptability is one of the traits Brian Decker sees in the most successful Special Operations soldiers. "If you think of the nature of Special Operations," Brian says, "what makes it unique is most of what you're asked to do is something you probably haven't seen before. You need to adapt from a base of knowledge and integrate all these specialized skills in innovative ways to accomplish your mission. That's what makes us humans special—the ability to adapt."

Adaptability is required in the business world because job functions are always evolving. The world is changing at an unbelievable pace, and you never know what's going to happen next. You need people who can adapt to whatever changes may come.

The job you're hiring for today will look different three, five, or ten years from now. "As you think about your candidate," says

CHRO Don Robertson, "you have to think about someone who not only can do the role as it is today but who also has the capability and mindset to grow and adapt."

Ultimately, you don't want cogs in a machine—robots capable of completing a single task. You want adaptable people who can step up and do whatever is needed.

## HUMILITY

People often ask us, "What is the most important trait of any leader?" Without a doubt, to us, it's humility. The US Army, a 244-year-old institution credited with training some of our nation's most prominent leaders and practically writing the leadership manual for leaders in any field, recently added *humility* as one of the key attributes of good leaders to the Army Doctrine Publication (ADP) 6-22, saying, "A leader with the right level of humility is a willing learner, maintains accurate self-awareness and seeks out others' input and feedback."[13]

Humility is the antidote to arrogance. Someone with appropriate humility recognizes that they do not have all the answers and that the aggregate intelligence and experience of everyone below and around them always far outweighs their own knowledge and experience. They are conscientious of the perspectives and views of others to form more educated decisions.

---

13 Corie Weathers, "The Army Has Introduced a New Leadership Value. Here's Why It Matters," Military.com, December 27, 2019, https://www.military.com/daily-news/2019/12/27/army-has-introduced-new-leadership-value-heres-why-it-matters.html.

Mike likes to joke that he's allergic to people who aren't humble. People without humility simply do not do well in Special Operations, or *any* team, because they prioritize themselves. In contrast, individuals with high humility recognize that they are simply one member of a larger, more important team, regardless of whatever their title is. As such, they tend to be selfless, putting the needs of the organization and others above themselves.

Someone with high humility also understands that, no matter how talented they are, victory is never guaranteed. Humility gives a person the ability to look in the mirror and do a brutal self-assessment. It prevents them from becoming complacent. Humility can counter what military leaders refer to as the "disease of victory." Throughout the history of warfare, there have been examples of military units beating their opponents multiple times in a row, growing more arrogant and more complacent with each victory. Overconfident, they charge into battle again, certain of victory, only to lose. With humility, an individual understands that just because they're successful once, twice, or even a dozen times in a row doesn't mean they own the keys to success.

As a quick caveat, humility is not the same thing as low self-confidence. Ego and pride are both useful, as they can drive people to do amazing things. There must be a balance of ego and humility. When someone's ego begins telling them that they know everything and cannot learn from anyone, the scale is tipping toward arrogance, making them a danger to themselves and the organization. Similarly, if someone always caves to others and does not trust their own expertise, the scale is tipped to low self-confidence, not true humility.

Retired SEAL Master Chief Jason Tuschen specifies that you want to search for "confident humility," which is when "a person realizes that they make mistakes and have weaknesses that they struggle to overcome, but they're confident that they can plow through it, either through teamwork or through grit and perseverance." One of the benefits of confident humility, he says, is that people are "confident and humble enough to ask for help when they know they are struggling."

In our experience, those with humility accomplish more than those without it, both because they understand that they always have more to learn and because they are willing to ask for help.

## INTEGRITY

Someone with integrity understands what is legal and what is right and aligns their actions and words with both. *Integrity is not optional.*

High performance without integrity is dangerous and will backfire eventually, like it did with Enron and Wells Fargo. In *The War for Talent*, Enron was held up as an example of good talent acquisition and talent development practices. The same month the book was published, October 2001, the Enron scandal came to light. Through unethical practices, the company had hidden billions of dollars of debt. The seemingly high-performing company filed for bankruptcy and never recovered, ruining the lives of thousands and severely impacting the energy sector and US economy.

Several years ago, Wells Fargo was involved in a staggering fraud scandal involving the creation of millions of fake checking and savings accounts without customers' consent. After the fraud came to light, not only did Wells Fargo lose many customers and significantly damage its reputation, but the US government also fined the company $3 billion—the cost of a lack of integrity.

In contrast, the US military is one of the most ethical organizations in the country. The bar for integrity is set higher for the military than for the business world, and for Special Operations Forces, the bar is even higher. Some people view SOF soldiers like cowboys of the Wild West—able to do whatever they want. The truth is that SOF operators are under the microscope even more, both in battle and at home. They have to be cautious about their actions and words because everything they do is dissected and scrutinized. When a Special Operations soldier makes an ethical mistake, it is front-page news that reflects poorly on the entire organization and could even have negative strategic impacts for our nation. As such, it is absolutely critical that each SOF operator possesses high integrity.

In Special Operations, candidates are often ranked in a *trust versus performance matrix*, a concept brought to prominence by Simon Sinek:

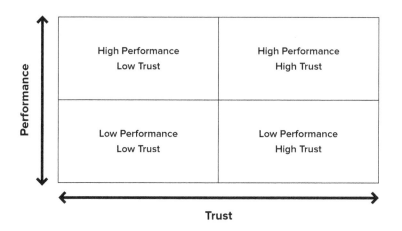

117

A candidate who is a medium performer with high trust is preferable to a candidate who is a high performer with low trust, because low-trust candidates can have toxic, damaging effects on the team and the culture.

Ethics violations do still occur in the military. No organization is perfect, because they're ultimately led by humans, and humans are flawed. However, the military deals with ethics violations very harshly. What you reinforce as an organization becomes the culture. By establishing clear ethical standards and severe consequences for breaking those standards, the military has built a culture of ethical behavior. For most, this sense of integrity stays with service members even after they leave the military, with research showing that veteran-led organizations tend to be more ethical than their counterparts.

Joe DePinto, CEO of 7-Eleven and former West Point graduate and Army officer, is a good example of how military-level integrity can be translated into the business world. "Having that compass that's pointing true north and sticking with your values and your principles that you stand for is critically important," he says.

Somebody who is going to step on others or break the law to succeed is not somebody you want in your company. People like that are generally not pleasant to work with, and they can prove to be very expensive. While they may produce results in the short term, their behavior and toxic leadership will damage if not destroy the organization in the long term, as seen in the cases of organizations like Enron, WorldCom, and Arthur Andersen LLP. Aside from creating astronomical legal bills, ethics violations can also damage your company brand and your customers' trust, which carries a cost of its own. Additionally, Dr. Josh Cotton has found in his research that the level of integrity in an organization is one of the most predictive metrics of turnover—specifically, if employees are not able to agree with the statement "I can report ethics violations without fear of reprisal," there will be high turnover.

## EFFECTIVE INTELLIGENCE

Raw intelligence is an important attribute that both sof and many successful chros prioritize. Tracy Keogh says, "For us, it starts with intellectual horsepower. We want super-smart people," and Don Robertson ranked intelligence in his top three traits for new talent.

ltc Brian Decker also pointed to intelligence as one of the best predictors of success. "Special Operations soldiers who are smart statistically do better in training," he says. "With a good test and measurement, we were able to better determine where that line [for iq] should be."

This is a very important qualifier: intelligence is important, *to a point*. Just as there are physical minimum requirements in Special Operations, there are also mental minimum requirements. *After meeting that minimum—the "line"—increasing levels of intelligence do not predict increasing levels of performance.* Brian said that in Army Special Operations, for enlisted, they would flag individuals at 110 iq, which is around the 75th percentile, and for officer consideration, they would flag at 115 iq, which is around the 85th percentile. A candidate with 125 iq would not necessarily be more successful than one with 110, so after a group of candidates met the minimum standard, IQ was no longer factored into the selection process.

It is also important to make sure that the metric you're looking at actually measures *intelligence*. GPA, for instance, isn't a good indicator of intelligence. Many people with high effective intelligence are only average students. The average college GPA of most millionaires is 2.9, and most leaders had an average GPA of 2.9 to 3.2.[14]

You want to search for *effective* intelligence, not high IQ. As MARSOC defines it, effective intelligence is the ability "to solve practical problems when a 'book solution' is not available" and to "learn and apply new skills to unusual problems by making sound and timely decisions." Effective intelligence is a person's ability to apply their knowledge to real-world scenarios. Someone could have a genius-level IQ, but if they don't know how to *apply* their knowledge in a conscientious way, it's useless, especially on the battlefield and in business, where time to make decisions and act is a luxury you can't afford. People with strong effective intelligence have high situational awareness. They are able to act with the appropriate action or inaction given ambiguous circumstances, and they are strong problem solvers.

Mike's experience within the SEALs and Joint Special Operations Command reinforces the necessity for effective intelligence. It's about the ability to solve problems, in a timely manner, with an incomplete picture. Many times, he and his team only had 50 to 70 percent of the operational picture or required information to

---

14  Shana Lebowitz, "Why Valedictorians Rarely Become Rich and Famous—and the Average Millionaire's College gpa Is 2.9," *Entrepreneur*, May 30, 2017, https://www.entrepreneur.com/article/295095.

conduct operations. All the SEALs he served with were of above-average intelligence or higher, regardless of the rank insignia they wore on their collar. In fact, most of his enlisted counterparts had multiple master's degrees before he even went to grad school. They did have off-the-charts intelligent SEALs. Some were effective because they possessed high situational awareness and the ability to keep solutions simple. But there were a good deal of the off-the-charts intelligent SEALs who couldn't apply their intelligence effectively for one of two reasons: (1) they suffered from "paralysis through analysis," often induced by not having all the facts, and (2) they overcomplicated things to the point of failure. They didn't last long in the SEAL teams.

Problem-solving is the ability to find solutions to challenging barriers, often through innovative thinking. Problem-solving requires applying one's knowledge and trying new methods and strategies.

General Boykin points to problem-solving as a key trait that makes operators unique. "Problem solvers are agile. No matter what they encounter, they're going to figure it out," he says. "Yet there's a lack of problem solvers in a lot of industries. Even some of our other military units don't assess for problem solvers, because they give soldiers manuals that tell them how to do everything, from marching to conducting tactical operations."

General Boykin gave us an example of problem-solving in action. During the hunt for Manuel Noriega in Panama in 1989, General Boykin and his unit were launching operations multiple times a day, using slow-scan technology. "When you're chasing somebody," General Boykin told us, "it's a matter of seconds as to whether you get them or not. [The slow-scan technology] wasn't good enough...The lesson we learned from Panama was that we've got to have real-time, right-now intelligence that we can react to, and that intelligence has to come from an overhead platform. Satellites aren't going to do it."

After Noriega's capture, with this lesson fresh in their minds, a couple of soldiers were watching overhead traffic reports on TV and thought, *Why can't we do the same thing?* The simple answer was that the unit didn't have the right technology. "The military was stuck on antiquated platforms," General Boykin explained, "but we said, 'What the heck? We'll just go buy what we need.' The guys put a plan together for how to use this stuff, and they went out, found it, and bought it. This was commercial off-the-shelf technology, nothing fancy about it."

A few short years later, during American intervention in Somalia in 1993, General Boykin's unit mounted these sensors on helicopters. It was the key to them being able to find and capture Somali warlords and their senior lieutenants because it provided them with a real-time picture of where these targets were. "The military didn't provide us what we needed, but my operators went out and figured out how to do it."

This story is an apt example of not only problem-solving but the first SOF truth: humans are more important than hardware. With the right people, you can overcome hardware deficiencies.

Intelligence is critical, but it is important that it is paired with humility and drive. Intelligence without humility will give you arrogant people who believe they are the smartest person in the room and who won't listen to anyone. Intelligence without drive will give you smart but lazy people who never rise to their full potential.

## TEAM-ABILITY

Nothing worth accomplishing can be done alone. There are no Rambos in the military. That might look cool in the movies, but individuals die pretty quickly on the battlefield or, worse, get others hurt. The greatest successes require that we work together. Captain Phillips of the *Maersk Alabama* wasn't rescued by one person, nor did the US Olympic hockey team win gold in 1980 because of a single player. Both endeavors required cohesive teams to win.

SEAL groups are called "teams" for a reason. You will often hear SEALS refer to themselves as "team guys." In all of Special Operations, teams are a way of life. This notion is driven into SOF candidates from day one. During SOF assessment, selection, and training, candidates are not allowed to execute any task or go anywhere without at least one teammate, often referred to as a "battle buddy" or "swim buddy." All SOF units are founded on an all-for-one team mentality. Team-ability is an individual's ability to function within a team, and it is a critical character attribute.

Teams aren't additive; they're multiplicative. If you have three people acting as individuals, they will output the work of three people. If, on the other hand, you have three people acting as a unified, cohesive *team*, they're going to output the work of more than three people. If you want to increase your company's productivity, you need to increase the cohesion of your teams.

In *Powerful*, Patty McCord says, "The most important job of management is to focus really intently on the building of great teams."[15]

---

15  Patty McCord, *Powerful: Building a Culture of Freedom and Responsibility...*

Building a great team requires hiring people with team-ability, because there is a difference between a group of people and a team. Just because five people report to the same boss doesn't make them a team. A team emerges when the members have *team-ability*, can prioritize organizational needs ahead of oneself, and work as a cohesive unit with one purpose: winning.

As Brian Decker says, "Adaptability and cooperation are the two things that separate us from every other animal on earth." Individuals can only accomplish so much. Teams have exponentially more potential.

## CURIOSITY

Curiosity—exploring the unknown and questioning the status quo in pursuit of better, more effective solutions—is the key to innovation. Without curious individuals, nothing would ever change or improve.

Curiosity is part of what General Boykin looked for during the assessment and selection of SOF candidates, precisely for this reason of innovation. "They had to be curious," he said. "They had to be the kind of people that wanted to explore things. That set the stage for figuring out how they could do something better."

People without curiosity stick to the status quo, with an attitude of "This is the way we've always done it, so it must be the right way." Special Operations soldiers cringe at the statement "This is the way we've always done it" or "This is tradition." Those words

---

...(Silicon Guild, 2018), 10.

imply inability to innovate and adapt and will quickly erode your reputation and credibility in the SOF community. Curious people understand that there's always a better way of doing things, and they explore and experiment until they find it.

Curiosity is especially critical because it is an indicator of future potential. We have no idea what roles or skills we'll need in the future, but you can count on someone with curiosity to learn what they need to. "My favorite people at HP," says Tracy Keogh, "are the people who are constantly reinventing themselves, the people who have been here for thirty years and still have fire in their bellies."

Like individuals with high drive, those with high curiosity will continue to grow and develop. Patty McCord points out in Powerful, "You've got to hire *now* for the team you wish to have in the future."[16] When you hire someone with curiosity, you're hiring them not just for who they are today but who they will become in the future.

## EMOTIONAL STRENGTH

In the US military, the "Whole Man" concept (detailed in the next chapter) is the belief that individuals need to be assessed based on the entirety of their person—mental, physical, and *emotional*. An emotionally strong individual has a positive attitude, high empathy, and emotional control in stressful situations.

Many of the individuals we interviewed identified positive attitude as important to their hiring decisions. Attitude is contagious.

---

16 Patty McCord, *Powerful: Building a Culture of Freedom and Responsibility* (Silicon Guild, 2018), 72.

Positivity breeds positivity, while negativity begets more negativity. An individual with a negative attitude can still produce results, but it is often at the expense of company culture. Typically, that one person's results are not worth the resulting damage to the team.

Any time teams are involved, empathy is another must. People often think of Special Operations soldiers as "tough, emotionless guys," but empathy is important to their success. As General Boykin explains, emotional intimacy is a necessity for a well-functioning team because it leads to trust. "If they lose a buddy, they're not afraid to let everybody see them weeping," he says, "because these guys have very close relationships. That fellowship and bond is important to cohesion and the total atmosphere of the team. It is key to what allows them to perform at the level they do because they're looking out for each other." The ability to build genuine relationships in the military is critically important to success, and it's equally important in the business world. With compassionate relationships, people feel like part of a team and are motivated to contribute the full extent of their talents.

Before you call SOF soldiers "special snowflakes," understand that simply possessing empathy is not enough in Special Operations; you must be able to adjust your level of empathy to what is needed by the situation—"empathy on a dimmer switch," as Rich Diviney explains it. "The ability to go to war and operate effectively depends upon being able to dial down empathy in the moment and do the job. Then, once the job is finished, you can dial the empathy back up to process and mourn what you have witnessed, to stay human. When people aren't able to effectively manage their empathy, either always remaining high empathy or always low empathy, you start seeing the infection of PTSD or unethical behavior."

Rich also points to the importance of vulnerability, saying, "Every high-performing team needs vulnerability. It's all about wearing your strengths and weaknesses on your sleeve. If I'm with you in combat, you have to know what I'm bad at, as well as what I'm good at, so that you then know where to pick up the slack. And I do the same with you."

The final marker of emotional strength is the ability to regulate one's emotions to remain logical under stressful conditions. MARSOC calls this stress tolerance and defines it as the "ability to deal with ambiguous, dangerous, high pressure and/or frustrating events while maintaining control of emotion, actions, composure, and effectiveness." It is a universal truth in life that humans don't make good decisions in an emotional state. People who are able to remain cool, calm, and collected in the face of challenges and the unknown are people you want in your organization. This is the exact reason SOF creates stressful environments, to mimic the conditions of war during assessment and selection programs. Stress tolerance is so important that some SOF organizations even use heart-rate monitors to evaluate individuals' physiological responses to stress.

Like each of the other nine traits, emotional strength alone is not enough to mark a candidate as high-potential. In a perfect world, you would be able to find candidates who possess a solid foundation in all nine characteristics, but that's not realistic. Instead, you must prioritize and weight the characteristics according to your particular organization and the individual role.

In the next chapter, we'll discuss how to do just that by assessing your top performers. We'll also cover how to create a strategic plan for your talent acquisition through workforce planning.

## KEY TAKEAWAYS

- We define talent—high-potential individuals—as those possessing drive, resiliency, adaptability, humility, integrity, effective intelligence, team-ability, curiosity, and emotional strength.
- Drive is the need for achievement, with a strong growth mindset.
- Resiliency is the ability to persevere in the face of challenges and bounce back from setbacks.
- Adaptability is the ability to adjust according to the situation, learn new things, and try new methods.
- Humility is a person's self-confidence in their own ability while understanding that they don't know everything and are always a work in progress.
- Integrity is an adherence to not only what is legal but also what is right.
- Effective intelligence is the ability to apply one's knowledge base to real-world scenarios and problem-solve.
- Team-ability is how well an individual functions as part of a team, placing the needs of the organization above their own.
- Curiosity is a desire to discover new information, continually learn more, and improve upon products, processes, and procedures.

- Emotional strength is having a positive attitude, high empathy, and the ability to regulate one's emotions when under stress.

Special Forces candidates assigned to the US Army John F. Kennedy Special Warfare Center meet with role players acting as village leaders during the final phase of field training, known as Robin Sage, in central North Carolina. Robin Sage is the culmination exercise and has been the litmus test for soldiers striving to earn the Green Beret for more than forty years.

*Source: Defense Visual Information Distribution Service / K. Kassens*

# CHAPTER 6

# KNOW THYSELF: CREATING A TALENT ACQUISITION PLAN

erseverance. Team player. Adaptability. Personal responsibility. Integrity. Courage. Professionalism. Capability.

These are the eight attributes Army Special Forces uses as the benchmark to select its Green Berets. Seeking to evaluate candidates across all of these attributes in combination with a measure of IQ (in this case the ASVAB) and physical ability is a method the military calls the "Whole Man" concept, as this method was designed to evaluate the entirety of an individual—mental, physical, and emotional. Although some form of this has always existed, evaluating candidates based on the Whole Man concept is now formally common practice throughout Special Operations.

Army Special Operations Forces (ARSOF) identified these core attributes by looking within the organization. Driven by a talent mindset, a group of high-performing Green Berets gathered around a table and asked, "What makes our most successful guys successful?" Through much discussion and debate, they settled on the eight ARSOF attributes. With more research and experimentation, they were able to develop assessments and processes to accurately identify those traits in candidates. However, they quickly discovered that attempting to assess for all eight traits at once was impractical. Plus, finding candidates who scored highly in every single trait was impossible. So, they zeroed in on the four traits that they felt were the strongest predictors of future success: perseverance (or resiliency), team player (team-ability), adaptability, and personal responsibility (or extreme ownership).

In the previous chapter, we outlined the nine core character attributes of talent—drive, resiliency, adaptability, humility, integrity, effective intelligence, team-ability, curiosity, and emotional strength. Each Special Operations arm of the military looks for some combination of these traits (though the vernacular they use may be different). For each branch, the most important traits vary slightly. The SEALS look for drive, team-ability, and resiliency. The Marines look for effectiveness under stress (which is related to resiliency) as well as decision-making and problem-solving ability (related to effective intelligence).

Think of it like a dartboard. Your candidates are only going to hit so many bull's-eyes. Since each candidate will hit dead center on only a few traits, you need to identify which traits are most important for each function and level within your company. However, candidates should at least be hitting the board with each dart, or trait. The Special Operations community has long believed in the idea of "jack of all trades, master of none." The person who exhibits the qualities of the "Whole Man" is not perfect, but they are well-rounded.

After you know what you *want* in talent, you must analyze what you are *missing* in your company. You must engage in thorough, constant workforce planning, with an emphasis on succession planning to identify the gaps in leadership and talent that need to be filled. It all starts by defining greatness within your organization.

---

### THE "WHOLE MAN" CONCEPT[17]

In the US military, the "Whole Man" concept is used to design personnel screening processes and remind evaluators that hiring and promotion decisions need to be based on everything the person is, not just one or two metrics, such as degrees earned or years of experience.

The Whole Man concept gained national attention because of the work of Harvard professor Dudley Sargent in 1880 when he built a program advocating that public education should include physical education. Prior to his work, US education saw little focus on the physical side. Sargent's motivation was based on a Greek ideal, *mens sana in corpore sano*, meaning "a healthy mind in a healthy body." Professor Sargent believed that to

---

17  US Special Operations Command, "Tip of the Spear," July 2005, https://www.socom.mil/TipOfTheSpear/July%202005%20Tip%20of%20the%20Spear.pdf.

produce productive citizens, education needed to focus on mental, spiritual, and physical growth.

Later, in the 1960s, the military began using the Whole Man concept to select airmen and sailors for promotion and at some entry points, such as the US Naval Academy. The military wanted to ensure that people were being evaluated as people and not simply based on achievements or education.

In World War II, the Office of Strategic Services, a precursor to Special Operations units and the CIA, was the first military unit to formally incorporate the Whole Man concept into military applicant selection for combat roles. While effective intelligence was a critical requirement, the men they selected needed to be highly well-rounded, as they would be dropped behind enemy lines and expected to blend in with the local populace in Africa, Europe, and Asia.

While the US military had been using the Whole Man concept since the early twentieth century, in 2005 the US Army Special Forces announced their intention to launch a large-scale study to enhance and formally utilize the Whole Man concept to expand how they evaluated candidates and ensure they measured applicants in all of the following areas: intelligence, trainability, judgment, influence, physical fitness, and motivation. They brought in psychologists, combat veterans, and top performers to first define what they were looking for. The product they were assessing were the high-performing operators at the active Special Forces Groups, engaged in day-to-day combat with enemy forces or coordinating strategic-level initiatives with other interagency organizations.

Today, the Whole Man concept still plays an important role, guiding how Special Operations selects and assesses its operators.

## DEFINE GREATNESS IN YOUR ORGANIZATION

While in charge of assessment and selection for a highly selective and specialized SEAL Team, retired Navy SEAL Commander Rich Diviney was tasked with determining why certain individuals succeeded and others failed. "Seemingly outstanding candidates would fail," he explained, "and we wanted to know why. Ultimately, we discovered that we were looking at and evaluating the wrong things. The things we thought made someone an outstanding candidate were, in fact, not indicators of future performance."

Every organization wants great people, but if you do not define what greatness is within your respective organization, you will be looking for the wrong things. As the Society for Human Resource Management advises, "In using any method for hiring new employees, one of the first things that an employer needs to determine is what exactly it is looking for in candidates."[18] If you don't know what

---

18 "A Guide to Conducting Behavioral Interviews with Early Career Job Candidates," *Society for Human Resource Management*, 2016, p. 4, https://www.shrm.org/LearningAndCareer/learning/Documents/Behavioral%20Interviewing%20Guide%20for%20Early%20Career%20Candidates.pdf.

you're looking for, of course you will struggle to hire effectively.

Part of the issue is that HR departments are many times disconnected from the business and, therefore, rarely know what success looks like for any given function in their organization. Frequently absent is a company- or function-specific definition of talent—those characteristics that high performers possess. Other times, the definitions exist, but they are simply words hung on the wall or posted on a website, and they are not actually used in the hiring process.

If no one has defined what success looks like in a role, you shouldn't post the job yet. When you skip this key step, screening criteria tend to be based on a job description as opposed to the desired talent of high performers. For instance, if a company is hiring for a salesperson, they will formulate their screening criteria around the generic skills of sales—years of experience, degree, and so on—as opposed to focusing on the traits that make their particular salespeople successful. Some companies need salespeople to be fast and technical. Others need them to be friendly and patient. If you don't define what you're truly looking for, your hiring won't be as effective as it could be.

We've provided you with a foundational definition of talent and outlined some of the most important attributes, but every company is unique and has its own dynamics. Just as the different Special Operations branches emphasize different character traits, each company will have its own picture of talent. To identify the core attributes most important for your organization, we recommend using the same strategy the US Air Force PJs and CCTs, Army Special Forces and Rangers, MARSOC Raiders, and Navy SEALs used to develop their lists: look within and evaluate your top performers.

"You have to figure out your winning formula," says CHRO Tracy Keogh. "You create the profile of talent based on your most stellar people." This isn't just talk for Tracy. In the past few years at HP, her department has completed about thirty-five thousand talent reviews of their top people. Only the best, most forward-thinking organizations will take the time and do the work required to truly understand their top talent.

It's important to assess your top performers because, as LTC Brian Decker says, "It's not always about getting the best person; it's about getting the right person." The best person may be the one with the shiniest resume, while the right person is the one with the character attributes and mindset that will allow them to succeed in the role.

By creating **talent profiles**—detailed descriptions of what talent looks like at every level of the organization and for each specific role/function, based on character traits—you can better search for the right person, not just the best person. The first step to creating these talent profiles is identifying your high performers.

## IDENTIFY YOUR HIGH PERFORMERS

To create profiles for talent, first identify your high performers at each level. These are the people that have navigated your unique organization—its tools, its processes, its people—and they are winning, so they should be your model for talent.

One easy way to identify your high performers is through performance metrics. The people who consistently meet or exceed their goals in any particular performance management system tend to be your top talent.

However, the objective or measurable data of metrics only provide part of the picture. You could have someone who excels in all the KPIs but is a terrible team player and contributes to a disruptive work culture. If you are not using the Whole Man concept, this person will get promoted. However, that is not the kind of person you want setting the standard for talent. While they may deliver results in the short term, their toxicity will come at the expense of the organization in the long term. On the other end of the spectrum, a rising star may have average metrics because they're still learning the ropes. That person could still be a great model for their role's talent profile because they have the character traits needed for success.

Even more than metrics, you should look at *reputation*. In SOF, reputation is everything. It is an indicator of how high performers work with and treat others. A high performer that fails to hold the trust of those around them—what the SOF communities refer to as "high-performing, low-trust"—is not the talent you want to emulate. You want people with good reputations—high-performing, high-trust people.

Ultimately, the people in your organization know who the talent is. Start by using available ratings in your performance system but also ask your managers to identify their best people. We also highly recommend using 360 surveys, which include peer evaluations. (To be even more effective, gather feedback from peer levels *outside* of the silo in which the evaluated person works.) Every SOF branch uses peer reviews in some capacity during assessment and selection processes because they provide a balanced insider's view of an individual. People are on their best behavior around their bosses, but their true character often comes out around their peers. Plus, if you have a manager who lacks a talent mindset or fears being out-shined by their followers, peer ratings can be more accurate than the manager's ratings.

## ASSESS YOUR TALENT

To build your talent profiles, both subjective and objective assess-ments should be used. In a subjective assessment, like a focus group or survey, people discuss and identify the key attributes based on the opinions of subject-matter experts. In objective assessments, a written tool, typically a multiple-choice personality and perfor-mance-assessment test is used to identify an individual's traits.

We recommend building your talent profiles based on your top performers, but consider assessing your poor performers too. It's usually from the bad hires that we learn the most, as failure often teaches us more than success. Just as high performers share attri-butes that point to talent, poor performers may share traits that predict their lower performance.

Start with the subjective. Subjective assessments should be the starting point because they provide you with a narrowed scope that you can then confirm and quantify with objective assessments. The important traits of talent—like drive, resiliency, and humil-ity—present in many different ways, which makes it difficult for objective tests to identify these attributes in the right amounts for your specific company.

We, of course, highly recommend that your talent profiles be closely aligned with the character traits we outlined in the previ-ous chapter. While we believe these character traits are universal,

139

regardless of the industry, every company will define the key attributes of talent a little bit differently and vary somewhat in the degree of that trait needed.

In assessing your top performers, you may identify an important attribute that we have not mentioned—like mathematical reasoning for a role in the financial sector or strategic thinking for enterprise-wide program designers. So it's important to assess your A-players to build your own talent profiles.

## SUBJECTIVE ASSESSMENTS

After identifying your top performers, the first step of assessing them should be subjective. Just like the Green Berets did, gather a focus group to answer the question, "What makes our most successful people so successful?"

Subjective assessments are most effective when they combine leader feedback with peer feedback, so you should have two separate focus groups: one composed of the managers for that role and one composed of the high performers in that role.

In preparation for the focus group, the participants should write down their thoughts ahead of time. This will help reduce bias, allowing the participants to form their opinions without influence.

As part of this preparatory "homework," tell the participants to think about what makes someone successful in the role being discussed—what separates the good employees from the great ones. Encourage them to think beyond hard skills. Ask them for stories and examples of employee success in the role, and then ask them to identify the fundamental character attributes that led to that success.

In the focus group, have everyone share their thoughts. There should be a focus group leader (generally an HR business partner) to manage the discussion and probe deeper when necessary, asking participants to give examples or explain what they mean by the words they choose, especially when discussing character attributes.

As you gather all this information, look for commonalities and patterns. Each high performer is going to look a little different, but they will share some traits, and those are the traits you must zero in on. Those attributes are the ones you will later use as predictors for success in the hiring process.

Once you have a solid subjective talent profile, you can move on to objective assessments.

## OBJECTIVE ASSESSMENTS

In Special Operations, many different objective assessments are used. There are physical assessments, like timed runs or pull-ups, and also aptitude assessments, such as the ASVAB, which is similar to the SAT or ACT and is mainly used to determine a candidate's eligibility for different occupations or specialties in the military. SOF also uses more overt intelligence testing, such as the Multidimensional Aptitude Battery II (MAB-II).

For most organizations, it is not practical or financially possible to create their own assessment. Fortunately, there are many existing objective assessments available for businesses. Naturally, some are better than others. It can be challenging to weed through the flashy marketing and find an effective assessment.

In general, there are two measures of an effective objective assessment:

- Does it measure what it says it's measuring?
- Does it measure something relevant?

As long as you begin with a subjective assessment, you will already know what attributes you want the assessment to identify and confirm. Thus, it will be easy to determine whether the test you are considering measures something relevant.

Determining whether an assessment measures what it says it is measuring can be more difficult. This is another great reason to begin with a subjective assessment. If you have twenty-five individuals you've identified as possessing high drive, then when they take the same objective assessment, most of them should score well in drive. If they don't, that assessment is not measuring what you want it to.

Next, examine the assessment's baseline comparison pool. Before bringing an assessment to market, the creators should have "tested the test," meaning they administered it to a pool of test subjects to ensure that it works as it should. Look at both how many and what kinds of people were included in the baseline pool. If the test pool is small, the assessment may not be as effective as it appears, and if you want to use an assessment to help identify leaders, then an assessment administered primarily to individuals in entry-level roles is not ideal.

Also pay attention to the disclaimers attached to assessments. Many of the most popular assessments—like DISC, Myers-Briggs, and StrengthsFinder—all carry disclaimers that they are *not pre-dictive* and should not be used to screen applicants. This means that they are not guaranteed or even intended to be used to indicate high potentials in the hiring process. The goal of administering objective assessments to your top talent is to pinpoint which assessments you can later use in the hiring process to predict post-hire job success. If an assessment is not predictive, it won't help you screen applicants.

You should be as particular about selecting your assessment test as you are about selecting a new hire. Only use assessment tests that say they can be used in hiring. Based on our personal experience, Elite Performance Indicator (a personality and competency assessment created by Dr. Josh Cotton), Hogan Assessments, and the Leadership Circle are worth your consideration. These assessments can provide valuable, scientifically driven information. But remember that subjective assessments must come first to ensure the assessment you are considering is a good fit for your company.

## BUILD YOUR TALENT PROFILES

After gathering both subjective and objective data, you need to *prioritize* and *weigh* which attributes to focus on in the same way that ARSOF prioritizes four of the eight total Whole Man attributes.

Which attributes you prioritize will vary according to job role and level. A top salesperson will look different from a top engineer, who will look different from a top general manager. Somebody on the manufacturing line may be the most successful if they regularly look for guidance from their bosses. Somebody in your IT department, on the other hand, may be more successful if they are a self-learner, able to solve problems on their own. Both may require a never-quit mentality to persist in solving problems where others give up. Study your top performers across the entire company—from the manufacturing line to the sales department to the C-suite—and create role-specific talent profiles where possible.

Remember the fifth SOF truth: Most Special Operations Forces require non-SOF assistance. All supporting business functions and all departments are crucial to your business's success. You want to have A-players at all levels.

Building talent profiles for every level will help give you a clear picture of how to identify viable, high-potential candidates in the hiring process. For your hiring process to be the most effective, you also need to engage in succession planning to determine what your company needs in terms of talent.

## WORKFORCE PLANNING

Every business plan must include talent planning. You won't get where you want to go without the right people, and as is true in business and life, lack of planning in any area often leads to poor, unintended, or disastrous results. *If you don't plan for talent, you are planning to fail.*

*"A lot of CEOS don't give a second thought to recruiting," says CHRO Tom Lokar. "It's a tactical thing that happens. They don't think about it strategically."*

After you identify the attributes you want in new talent, you must determine where you need new talent within your organization. That requires workforce planning. The Special Operations community and the military as a whole have created systems and processes to continually assess their talent pools, gaps, and succession plans, as the defense of our nation and their capability in responding to emergencies depends on their ability to maintain a competent and qualified force.

First, you need to identify single points of failure—skills or job functions without any redundancy. Some companies call these "critical roles." If you're in the tech field, for instance, and you have only one person on staff who knows a certain programming language, that is a single point of failure. If that critical employee gets sick, takes a vacation, or leaves the company, who steps up to fill that role? You should never be in a position where the loss of a single person creates a vacuum in your organization.

Second, because the business world is a grow-or-die environment, you need to examine what competencies you have today in your organization and what competencies you will need in the future. In the military, failing to understand and plan for your organization's future is an error called "fighting the last war." Once a war is over, it's time to start planning for the future wars and stop fighting the last one. Future wars, like future market conditions, will be completely different and require a different set of competencies to win.

In business, to stop "fighting the last war," you need to do a forward-thinking gap analysis, determining what you need but don't have. Ask yourself, "Who do I have today, and are they the right people to get me to tomorrow?" It is critical that your talent plan is closely connected to your business strategy. Maybe the plan is for the company to become more customer-centric in the future or to adapt to the digital economy. Do you have the right talent in place for your company's future? If not, you need to factor that into the talent profile of what you're looking for in new hires. Rather than hiring for a role as it is today, you need to forecast what that role is going to look like—what are you going to need in the way of talent for now and for the future?

With better workforce planning, you can help prevent the need for mass hires, as happened to George with the company that started a brand-new division without proper workforce planning, as detailed in chapter 2. If you don't adequately plan ahead and you find yourself in a position of suddenly needing to hire five hundred hard-to-find people in three months, you've made a strategic mistake. Remember the fourth SOF truth: competent Special Operations Forces cannot be created after emergencies occur. Mass hires are a type of emergency, and they will likely force you to compromise quality, violating the second SOF truth: quality is better than quantity. As Don Robertson says, "You have to be intentional and proactive in your hiring plans, and they have to be tied back to your workforce plans."

## LOOK AT SUCCESSION

One of the most critical parts of workforce planning is succession planning for your key leaders. Succession planning prepares you for the inevitable changes in leadership and allows you to create mentorship and development programs to nurture leaders within your organization so that you can promote from within instead of looking externally.

External sourcing of talent has value, but it's expensive, contains potential risk to your culture, and is a missed opportunity to reward your high-performing workers. Rewarding high performers creates even more high performers. Part of having a talent mindset means building an environment where top talent is rewarded with increasing responsibility and pay.

Succession planning is not something you can do once a year. At Hewlett-Packard, says Tracy Keogh, they "talk about succession planning in every meeting." Your organization is a living, breathing entity that is constantly changing, and so your succession plan must constantly change too.

In the military, especially Special Operations, succession planning is so ingrained, it is like muscle memory. It is one of the things the military does better than nearly anyone else. On a micro level, in battle, you never know when a leader might be injured, killed, or otherwise incapacitated. If the leader is taken out, there must be a clear, competent second-in-command to step up and take the leader's place. And if that person is also taken out, there is a third leader, fourth leader, and so on. You could have a two-hundred-person unit, and there would be a succession plan down to that final two-hundredth soldier. In SOF, every operator on every mission is ready to take charge of the team if needed. Can you say the same in your company?

SOF succession planning includes annual fitness reports as well as periodic reviews of leaders. During reviews, senior community leaders assess the members of specific ranks against one another. (So, for example, all majors in the Special Forces community are compared to each other, but they are not compared to majors in logistics or in the tank community.) The members are then racked and stacked in order of performance. Those with the requisite ability are promoted, and those who show potential are earmarked for further development. With these annual reviews, the SOF community is able to properly allocate resources and put the right leaders into the right roles, accelerating the community's evolution.

Some businesses skip assessments and instead base leadership positions on employee tenure as opposed to ability. This is a poor strategy. "If you offer leadership positions as a reward for being with an organization for a long time," says General Boykin, "you're not going to have the best leadership."

A pay raise and title change do not magically make someone an effective leader. If you want the best leadership, you need to develop it, and in order to best develop it, you need to engage in regular succession planning to identify your future leaders and gaps within your talent pool. By engaging in robust, constant succession planning, Special Operations Forces ensure that professional development is designed in a way that elevates both the individuals and the organization as a whole. Due to diligent planning, they have key leaders in all the right spots, with others ready to step up when needed. If there are gaps, new talent is selected to fill them.

If you're not doing workforce and succession planning, you are saying that it's okay to have blind spots, that it's okay to not know your weaknesses or gaps. Too many companies don't think about what might happen if a key leader is promoted or quits until it happens. They might have a general idea of who their number two and number three are, but there is no detailed, written plan. If your organization does not have an explicit succession plan for all its key functions, a single leader leaving could be hugely detrimental. Through proper succession planning, you can be strategic about your hiring to fill gaps and prevent leadership and talent vacuums.

Succession planning involves asking questions like the following:

- What is the quality of our talent? Where are our gaps?
- What pillars of talent do we need now, and what building blocks do we need for the future?
- Where are we missing leadership? Where are we missing number twos and number threes?
- What do we need in terms of human capital over the next year? The next five years? The next ten years?
- In what areas are we growing? Which departments are set to expand and when?
- Where might we experience attrition? Who's a flight risk?

By answering these questions and completing gap analyses (both talent gaps and leadership gaps) at *all levels* of your organization, you can begin to make smarter hiring decisions.

---

## THE 9 BOX: A SUCCESSION-PLANNING TOOL

The 9 Box assessment tool is ideal for succession planning because it identifies employees' current and potential positions in the company.

---

| Low Performer High Potential | Moderate Performer High Potential | High Performer High Potential |
|---|---|---|
| Low Performer Moderate Potential | Moderate Performer Moderate Potential | High Performer Moderate Potential |
| Low Performer Low Potential | Moderate Performer Low Potential | High Performer Low Potential |

*Potential Axis*

**Performance Axis**

The 9 Box is a three-by-three grid of nine boxes. Most of the time the vertical axis measures performance, and the horizontal axis measures potential, though sometimes these are flipped. The top far right box thus indicates highest performance and highest potential. The people clustered at the top right of the box are poised for promotion into higher roles. The people at the bottom left, unless they're newly hired, require more training and leadership development, and in some cases need to be let go.

Everyone in a leadership role should complete the 9 Box, placing their direct reports where appropriate. If they don't have anyone in the top right corner, it indicates a significant leadership vacuum. If that leader should move out of their position for any reason, there would be no one to take their place.

Ideally, the CEO and all of the CEO's first-level direct reports will complete a new 9 Box every quarter, or every six months at a minimum. People in the 1 block (the top right block) are ready for advancement immediately, people in the 2 block (the top middle block) are typically ready for a higher role within six months, and people in the 3 block (the right middle block) need anywhere from six to eighteen months to be prepared for advancement. This gives you a clear picture of not only who is in line for succession but also how much professional development they need to advance.

In addition to identifying leadership gaps and people in need of development, the 9 Box also identifies flight risks. If you have many top performers crammed into the 1, 2, and 3 blocks and only a couple of promotions scheduled for the next year, then you know who may grow dissatisfied and begin looking for work elsewhere. Armed with that knowledge, you can either prepare for them to leave or take action to ensure they stay.

You should complete 9 Boxes regularly because people are constantly changing. An employee who once showed high leadership potential may turn out to be a poor fit, and one who showed lower leadership potential may grow and become an exceptional leader. You must regularly evaluate your people to identify who is ready to step into a higher role and who needs more development first.

# BUILD REDUNDANCY BY HIRING FOR GREATNESS

Once you've identified the leadership and talent gaps in your organization, you can begin building redundancy by hiring based on the
talent profiles you've created.

Redundancy is critical. Within Special Operations, there is
redundancy built into every level. For every critical skill, there are
multiple individuals who can execute it. In contrast, businesses
aim to be lean, leaving themselves with far more individual con-
tributors who can do work no one else can. That approach simply
would not work in Special Operations. For instance, if the com-
munications sergeant were an individual contributor and were to
be incapacitated, then the entire unit would be cut off from the
rest of the world, unable to communicate when lives are on the
line. That is an unacceptable situation, and so the redundancy is
built in.

Building redundancy should be a goal of your hiring process.
People move from job to job with far more frequency today than
ever before. One of your key leaders or your top-performing salesperson could leave at any moment. If you don't have leadership and
talent redundancy, your company could be set back months as you
try to fill the vacuum.

The need for redundancy is part of why we've identified adaptability as a key trait of talent. When you hire people who are adaptable, they can more easily move from role to role within your
organization to fill gaps, even if it requires learning new skills.

By hiring for redundancy, you can afford losses and movement
without a significant dip in performance.

By assessing your top performers and taking inventory of your organization, you can identify what talent looks like and where you need to build redundancy. Once you know what you're looking for in new hires, you can create a strategy to attract the right candidates, which we will cover in the next chapter.

## KEY TAKEAWAYS

- You can't hire talent if you don't know what talent looks like in your organization. Build *talent profiles* in your organization by assessing your top performers at every level of your organization.
- Identify the most important attributes of your top performers through subjective focus groups. Reinforce your findings with objective written assessments (personality and competency testing).
- Update your succession plan regularly, ideally every three months or every six months at a minimum.
- *Plan* your hiring needs. If you fail to plan, you are planning to fail!
- Build redundancy in leadership and talent so that you are prepared for any sudden departures, moves in your hierarchy, or growth.

Basic Underwater Demolition/SEAL (BUD/S) students participate in surf passage at Naval Amphibious Base Coronado. Surf passage is one of many physically and mentally demanding evolutions that are a part of the first phase of SEAL training.

*Source: Defense Visual Information Distribution Service / Kyle Gahlau*

# CHAPTER 7

# KNOW YOUR AUDIENCE: ATTRACTING TOP TALENT

ike Sarraille grew up in Atherton, California, one
of the most affluent towns in America, home to the
Silicon Valley elite. Though the area is a staunch supporter of our military, enlisting is an atypical path. Yet that is
what Mike chose to do, just like many other talented individuals
across the nation. The military and SOF, in particular, are talent
magnets, and businesses can learn a lot by studying how they
attract talent.

In Mike's case, the turning point was when he met a Marine Staff
Sergeant named Ben. Ben was a Force Reconnaissance Marine,
the Marine Special Operations–capable force from the late 1950s
until the creation of MARSOC (Raiders) in 2006. He was intelligent,

articulate, thoughtful, physically fit, and humbly confident. Mike immediately thought, *I want to be just like that man.* That encounter ultimately led Mike to join the Marine Corps.

When Mike entered Marine boot camp, he knew he was in the right place. The drill instructors reminded him of Ben. They demonstrated amazing discipline in every facet of their lives, something Mike found awe-inspiring. They were the kind of people Mike aspired to be, and it drove him through the process, making him want the title of Marine even more.

Mike successfully completed Marine boot camp and next attended the School of Infantry. A team of ten Recon Marines showed up to screen the class of 150 infantry students for a chance to try out for the Marine Basic Reconnaissance Course (BRC). It was like ten of Ben stepped in front of Mike. Again, Mike was struck by the thought, *That is who I want to be.* And so was his path determined, leading him to earn the title of Recon Marine. Later, Mike worked with a platoon of Navy SEALS and experienced the same sentiment once again. He then branched onto a different path, becoming a SEAL.

The military has long understood that you need to put your best in front of those seeking entrance into your organization. If you want to attract the best, you must show that your organization is a place where talent thrives. One of the best ways to do that is through your people.

Over the years, the quality of SOF candidates has increased exponentially. Today, more enlisted Special Operations candidates have bachelor's and master's degrees than in any previous era of Special Operations. Talented individuals, like Evan Hafer (Green

Beret and CEO/Founder of Black Rifle Coffee Company) and Dan Crenshaw (SEAL and US Representative from Texas) could choose to do anything, but time and time again, they chose to pursue Special Operations. Why? Because Special Operations understands what talent wants and knows how to market itself.

The talent is out there. It's up to *you* to find it, get it, and keep it. If you're not actively working to attract talent, it's time to start.

## WHAT TALENTED PEOPLE LOOK FOR

Attracting talent requires knowing what talented people want. Many companies assume that the answer is money and perks. They offer competitive salaries and wonderful creature comforts—high-end espresso machines, fully stocked kitchens, pool tables, and more—yet they still hemorrhage talent. On the other end, we've seen countless people turn down higher pay to stay with a company where they feel challenged and love the people they work with.

If you want people to dedicate their talents to your company, you must offer them something equally valuable in return. Since talented people have high drive, they are just as interested in achievement and challenge as money. Let's not fool ourselves—if your compensation and benefits are not competitive within your industry, you will lose out on talent, but attracting the top people goes beyond that. Beyond the money, talented people look for talented leaders and colleagues, a sense of community, challenge, opportunities for professional and personal growth, and purpose.

## TALENTED LEADERS AND COLLEAGUES

*Talent attracts talent.* Why do you think Special Operations and the top companies are talent magnets? "Great talent wants to work for great talent," says CHRO Tom Lokar. Talent is a self-fulfilling prophecy: the best talent makes the best organizations, which attract the best talent, which attracts yet more talent. Success begets success. The more you hire and develop talent, the easier it will be to attract talented candidates.

People are the glue that holds a company together. Many soldiers join the military out of patriotic duty, but on the battlefield, it's not patriotism that drives them; it's their fellow soldiers. When we asked one SEAL what he thought about during battle, he said, "We're thinking about each other. We're fighting for each other." More than any other factor, the people we work with dictate our level of job satisfaction, so of course, talented people will be drawn to other talent, particularly talented leaders.

Ultimately, people don't leave companies; they leave bosses. It is very difficult to leave a great boss, even if someone else is offering you more money. "You want to work with and for good people," LTC Brian Decker says. "You want to work for somebody who has a compelling vision and a strategy to achieve it."

On the other side, if leadership is terrible, it is difficult to get talented individuals to stay, even if the compensation is good. As CHRO Don Robertson says, "A-talent doesn't want to work for B-talent." A bad leader is highly destructive to the overall culture and ultimately your ability to attract and retain talent.

*Talented people have a wealth of options available to them, so they will not tolerate bad leaders.*

## A SENSE OF COMMUNITY

From a psychological perspective, most people join gangs or terrorist groups for the same reason most people join the Navy SEALs: they want to be part of a team. Two wildly different sides of the spectrum, good versus evil, but ultimately people in both organizations want the same thing. They want a sense of homecoming and belonging—what the Marine Corps refers to as "esprit de corps." They want to be part of an organization that will do anything for its people.

When people feel a sense of community, they are more loyal, and in today's corporate culture of people hopping from job to job, loyalty is more important than ever.

To feel like part of a community, people must feel they provide value to the community. To attract talent, you need to have a culture in which you clearly recognize people's achievements and make them feel valued.

## CHALLENGE

More than three hundred people have died trying to climb Mount Everest. Yet there's no shortage of people attempting the climb each year. Becoming a Navy SEAL or a Green Beret requires pushing your body past all physical and mental limits. The training has an 80 to 85 percent attrition rate and can break even elite athletes.

Who in their right mind would sign up for a year of hell with an 80 to 85 percent attrition rate? Yet year after year, there's no shortage of people who sign up for this opportunity to be broken down to their core. They stand in line and compete for the chance to run through fifty-two-degree water and have sand rub parts of their body raw. When we asked one SEAL why he signed up, he said, "It was the hardest thing I could think of."

This is part of what makes Special Operations and the best companies such great attractors of talent. They have zeroed in on this innate human drive that says, "I can do anything." There's no shortage of people who want to do the extraordinary, who want to challenge themselves physically, mentally, emotionally, and spiritually.

Attracting talented people means providing them with an environment in which they can make full use of their talents. As Don Robertson says, "You're not going to attract the best talent if you don't create an environment that requires the best talent."

You need to create the perception that your organization will offer a challenge—a chance to do the biggest, hardest, most dynamic, fastest-changing work that will ultimately set your workers up for success in every facet of their lives. Then you pose the challenge to potential talent: do you have what it takes?

## GROWTH OPPORTUNITIES, AUTONOMY, AND OWNERSHIP

Remember that talented people have high drive. They have a growth mindset and are always striving for more.

When talented people are looking for a new job, they are rarely looking to move laterally. They want to move up. They want responsibility and greater impact. They want to work toward bigger goals and grow, personally and professionally. They are interested in pushing the limits of what they can accomplish, so if they don't see clear growth opportunities at your organization, they will take their talents elsewhere.

Talented people also want autonomy—the ability to have some control over their own destiny. In other words, talented people want ownership—not necessarily an equity stake or an actual share of a company—but ownership that allows freedom—freedom to make decisions, freedom to plan, and freedom to execute. This should not be hard to achieve, since good leaders implement decentralized command, which is built on trusting subordinates with ownership and autonomy to make things happen. Talent feeds off of this leadership methodology.

Valuing talent gets you valuable talent. As we will discuss further in chapter 10, providing growth and development opportunities to your talent is one of the smartest choices you can make. Not only does it lower attrition, which saves you money, but it allows you to source talent for middle- to senior-level leadership positions within your company, as we discussed in chapter 6, "Know Thyself," in the section about succession planning.

## PURPOSE

Inspired people seek out inspiring organizations. Talented people want to know that their work matters—they want purpose.

"You want to work in a role where you can contribute value," says LTC Brian Decker. You can make all the money in the world, but if you're not having an impact, it doesn't matter. You will feel dissatisfied because a life without purpose is a life unfulfilled. The greatest currency in life is the impact you have on others.

People want to know their "why"—their purpose. In the military, one's purpose is easy to identify: defending and protecting one's nation. In the private sector, the importance of a role can be less clear. It is up to you to define the purpose you provide for your prospective employees. For example, a construction crew's purpose might be building homes for people, or an oil rig worker's purpose could be contributing to the country's energy independence. Even if the purpose is not immediately obvious, it does exist. Your company must fulfill some need in the world or your local community, or it wouldn't exist. You must identify that need and translate it to prospective employees.

Nobody wants to feel like their time and efforts are worthless, so as a company, you need to tell prospective employees what impact they can have by joining your organization.

## SALARY AND BENEFITS

Despite what some would have you think, money isn't everything, though it does play an important role. In a survey of sixteen thousand employees spread across the globe, Dr. Josh Cotton found that the people who were paid the most were not necessarily the ones who were the happiest or most engaged.

Especially for talented people with high drive, money is usually a concern up front but not the most important factor down the road. Special Operations soldiers handle highly classified material, regularly risk their lives, and have highly refined leadership skills, yet they are paid much less than senior-level managers in the corporate world. Similarly, many talented people choose to become teachers or nurses or any number of underpaid careers. What we have identified both in the military and private sector is that talented people find more satisfaction in challenge and purpose than money.

But let's be honest: pay matters. To attract talent, salaries and benefits must be reasonable or competitive for the market. You don't have to be at the top, but you certainly don't want to be at the bottom. You need to be in the ballpark.

## BRAND YOURSELF AS A TALENT MAGNET

The US military, especially Special Operations, has skillful marketing and branding. Their branding is successful because they have zeroed in on the importance of talent. You can see it in the different forces' slogans and mottoes over the years:

- The few, the proud, the Marines. (Marine Corps)
- Rangers lead the way. (Army Rangers)
- That others may live. (Air Force Pararescue)
- De oppresso liber (To free the oppressed). (Army Special Forces)
- The only easy day was yesterday. (Navy SEALS)

The military attracts talent because it *markets and calls to talented individuals.* Each of these slogans or mottoes points to something talent wants: talented leaders and colleagues, a sense of community, challenge, growth opportunities, or a sense of purpose.

Special Operations Forces, in particular, are a talent magnet because they offer everything high-performing people want. They provide a challenge and a chance to be a part of an elite team. They give recruits an important purpose, and the training and support needed to reach their fullest potential.

Most companies spend thousands marketing their products or services to customers, but they don't put enough time, energy, or money toward marketing to the right future employees. This is a huge—and costly—mistake. Remember: your greatest competitive advantage is not your product or service; *it's your people.* If you're not willing to dedicate the resources to market yourself to potential employees, how can you expect to attract the top talent?

You could have a great organization with great talent, but it doesn't matter unless people *know* it's a great organization. When hiring for talent, you are limited by your applicant pool. To increase the quality of your initial talent pool, you must brand yourself as a place for people to thrive and grow. That starts with a strong employee value proposition.

## EMPLOYEE VALUE PROPOSITION

An employee value proposition (EVP) is collectively what you, as an employer, offer to your employees. Essentially, your EVP is why someone would want to work for your company instead of anywhere else.

Here are two examples of EVPs and excerpts from the Navy SEAL Ethos and the Ranger Creed, which function like EVPs:

- PricewaterhouseCoopers (PwC): "From empowering mentorships to customized coaching, PwC provides you with the support you need to help you develop your career. You'll work with people from diverse backgrounds and industries to solve important problems. Are you ready to grow?"

- Google: "There's no one kind of Googler, so we're always looking for people who can bring new perspectives and life experiences to our teams. If you're looking for a place that values your curiosity, passion, and desire to learn, if you're seeking colleagues who are big thinkers eager to take on fresh challenges as a team, then you're a future Googler."

- Navy SEALs: "In times of war or uncertainty there is a special breed of warrior ready to answer our Nation's call. A common man with uncommon desire to succeed. Forged by adversity, he stands alongside America's finest Special Operations Forces to serve his country, the American people, and protect their way of life. I am that man."

- Ranger Creed: "Recognizing that I volunteered as a Ranger, fully knowing the hazards of my chosen profession, I will always endeavor to uphold the prestige, honor, and high esprit de corps of the Rangers. Acknowledging the fact that a Ranger is a more elite Soldier who arrives at the cutting edge of battle by land, sea, or air, I accept the fact that as a Ranger my country expects me to move further, faster and fight harder than any other Soldier...Rangers lead the way!"

Notice how these all mention at least one key thing talented people look for: good leaders and colleagues ("colleagues who are big thinkers"), a sense of community ("stands alongside America's finest Special Operations Forces"), challenge ("Are you ready to grow?"; "move further, faster and fight harder than any other Soldier"), growth opportunities ("the support you need to help you develop your career"), and defined purpose ("solve important problems"; "serve his country, the American people, and protect their way of life").

An EVP creates a perception of what it is like to work at your company. A good business EVP is typically composed of four parts: growth and development opportunities, work environment/culture, defined purpose, and monetary compensation / other benefits. When crafting an EVP, think about what your company offers to its employees in each of these areas. Ideally, what you offer will be what high-performing people want. If you imagine a Venn diagram of what you want and what talent wants, the section in the middle is the basis for your EVP.

Your EVP should be short, a single sentence or paragraph. It doesn't need to be complicated. It can be as simple as "We hire the best talent, and we let them be their best." Some EVPs focus on company values, and others concentrate on the nuts and bolts of benefits, compensation, and development. What matters is that your EVP resonates with your company and the talent you want to attract.

Once you have a clearly articulated EVP, it should be woven through your entire company, available to existing employees as well as potential hires. It should go on your website (either the main page or the career page) and should be included in all your job postings.

Periodically revisit your EVP every few years, or whenever you do a brand refresh. When you revisit your EVP, also look at whether it's effective in attracting the talent you want. This can be difficult to measure, but if you're consistently attracting the wrong kind of people, your EVP isn't doing its job.

## Employee Value Proposition

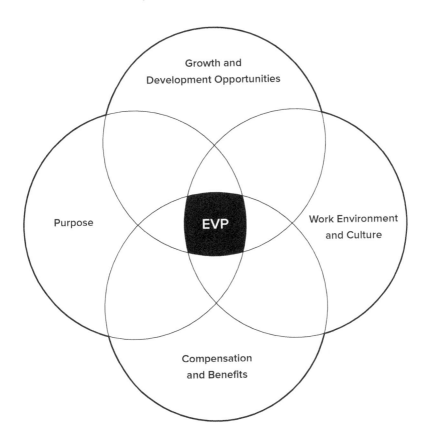

The most important thing to remember with your EVP is that the values you choose to highlight need to accurately reflect the culture that your leaders and people are driving, reinforcing, and inculcating every day in your company. Every organization preaches a mission and core values, but too often, they're just flowery words that sound good on paper. Your EVP can't be just words. It must be a code that you live by, in the same way that Navy SEALs live by their code: "Loyal to country, team, and teammates. Serve with honor and integrity, on and off the battlefield. Ready to lead, ready to follow. Never quit. Take responsibility for your actions and the actions of your teammates."

Even though he's retired from the military, Mike still carries a Naval Special Warfare (SEAL) Code of Conduct card in his wallet, imprinted with this code and the words "Earn Your Trident Every Day." The words mean something because he lives them. Retired or not, Mike truly believes that he represents the SEAL community every day through his actions. He seeks to conduct himself and represent his community in a way that inspires the younger generation to accept the challenge and join the SEALs or military. If you want your EVP to mean something, you must live it.

## GLASSDOOR

If a candidate wants to know more about your organization, one of the first places they will look is Glassdoor. Here are some tips for how to make sure Glassdoor is working to attract talented candidates, not repel them.

1. Encourage your top employees to submit reviews. Are your good employees bragging about your company? The number one problem with Glassdoor is that often only the squeaky wheels comment. You need your top talent to comment as well, to balance out the message. C-suite executives always complain to us about Glassdoor, yet few take the time to leave reviews themselves. Remember: if you want to drive a talent mindset in your organization, it must come from the top. If you want your employees to leave reviews, then lead by example.

2. Address negative comments. Many of the negative comments you receive on Glassdoor will be unfounded, left by people who have unrealistic expectations or who are bitter they didn't get the job. But some of the negative comments will be justified. Take ownership of them, especially if you see patterns or common themes. Use the comments as a way to improve your organization, then communicate on Glassdoor how you have addressed the feedback.

3. Build a good candidate interview experience. Often, negative reviews on Glassdoor are not about working at the organization but applying to work at the organization. Even if you don't ultimately hire a candidate, you want them to have a positive experience interviewing. You never want to burn bridges. In

chapter 9, "The Hiring Process," we will discuss tips and strategies for creating a good interview process.

## USING SOCIAL MEDIA TO REACH TOP TALENT

Using or not using social media is no longer an option. You don't have to like social media; you just have to accept it and utilize it to your advantage. Even US Special Operations Command (USSO-COM), known for being highly secretive in the past, has come to realize the power of social media and now has an Instagram page (@ussocom) as part of their recruiting efforts.

To attract the new generation of talent, you *must* use social media, but you also must be thoughtful about how you use it because it can have disproportionate effects. A single unhappy person can trigger a Twitter campaign of outrage. Mastering how you distribute your message over social media is an absolute imperative in the talent war.

The key with social media is to set the narrative for your company, which should be that you value talent. If you don't create your narrative, then in today's social media environment, someone else will set it for you, and you might not like their story.

One of the best ways to disseminate your talent mindset via social media is to focus on your employees. On the USSOCOM Instagram account, for instance, they post pictures of special operators in action, like Air Force Pararescue (PJS) rescuing somebody from the side of a mountain during training or Army Rangers conducting combat operations in Afghanistan. These images provide an inside look at what USSOCOM is while also highlighting the talent within the organization.

To provide an inside look into your organization, interview your top employees and ask what they love about your company and working there. Then post highlights from the interview with a photo or video. Candidates can then see that your talent mindset is not just words but a real part of your company. As an added bonus, the featured employees will feel valued and more bonded to your organization.

Effective social media marketing should accomplish two things: (1) showcasing your service or product and (2) showcasing your culture and the people behind the product or service. In this way, you can market your company on two levels: to customers and to future talent.

---

## TIPS TO MAXIMIZE LINKEDIN AND OTHER BUSINESS NETWORKING SITES

LinkedIn is, without a doubt, the number one platform for recruiters to find talent and for professionals to connect, ask questions, and investigate different industries. Often, it will provide the first impression a new candidate gets of your company. Here are three tips to maximize LinkedIn and similar sites.

1. Provide your employees with boilerplate material to add to their individual profiles on professional networking sites.

Your talent is your brand, and every employee is a representation of your company. With most companies, if you look at ten different employees' profiles, it will look like the company does ten different things. You can't—and shouldn't—dictate what your employees write on their profiles, but if you provide them with clear professional copy, most are grateful for the resource and happy to use it, which can help you send a consistent message.

2. Encourage your high-level leaders to be active on networking sites. Senior executives tend to have the sparsest profiles on LinkedIn, which is a mistake. LinkedIn is designed to link *people*, not companies. If a leader has a bare-bones profile, candidates will glance through it and leave. With a more-robust profile, where the leader represents your organization well, you could attract more talented individuals.

3. Make use of the recommendations feature. On everybody's LinkedIn profile, there is a section for recommendations given and recommendations received. Obviously, having recommendations is important, but giving recommendations can be even more powerful. Giving a recommendation to an employee on a public forum like LinkedIn is a way to recognize and reward their talent. It can

> elevate their career while simultaneously reinforc-
> ing that they're valued. Giving recommendations
> is also tangible proof of a talent mindset. Imagine
> somebody visits the LinkedIn profile of a CEO or
> CHRO and sees that they've given out more than a
> dozen recommendations to company employees.
> That is the kind of company talented individuals
> want to work for.

## DON'T WAIT FOR TALENT TO COME TO YOU

There are two kinds of employee candidates: active and passive. An active candidate is one who seeks you out, either applying through a job posting or contacting your organization directly. A passive candidate is one that you find and approach, typically through a recruiter.

Most companies rely on active candidates, which limits the pool of talent. Every company should recruit passive candidates, but it's even more important when you have limited brand recognition. If you're a Fortune 500 company like Google or Coca-Cola and you post a job opening, you will likely receive at least fifty qualified candidates. If you're a small, relatively unknown company, though, you might not receive any.

Even with the large number of people wanting to be Special Operations soldiers, SOF recruiters attend high school and college events to actively identify high-potential candidates and recruit them into Special Operations contracts. As another example, at

Forcepoint, the cybersecurity company where George serves as Global Head of Talent Acquisition, even though they have a strong product brand and attract good applicants, they put a lot of energy into strategic recruitment of passive candidates. Roughly 65 percent of their candidate pool comes from passive candidates, allowing them to hire and maintain a much higher standard for talent than if they relied on active candidates alone.

You must seek out talent. Don't be complacent and wait for it to come to you.

To be even more proactive, also engage in *opportunistic hiring*, where you're always looking for great talent, regardless of whether you have open positions.

## OPPORTUNISTIC HIRING

Companies that actively engage in opportunistic hiring are more equipped to respond to both growth and emergencies. Most companies hire only when they have vacant positions, but when there's an immediate demand, there is a time pressure that puts restrictions on how effectively you can identify and select talent.

Opportunistic hiring is the practice of hiring good talent whenever the opportunity arises, instead of waiting for an open position. A talented individual represents an opportunity for your company, and when opportunity knocks, you answer the door. If you only hire to fill vacant positions, it's the equivalent of ignoring all the knocks on your door; then, when you finally have a position to fill, you open the door and hope you happen to find talent on the other side.

The best companies are always hiring, even if there is not a specific role to be filled. In *Good to Great*, Jim Collins compares a business to a bus and discusses the importance of getting the right people in the right seats. When you find top talent, your priority should be getting them on the bus. You can worry about finding them the right seat later. Even if all the seats are currently filled, it's better to have talent on the bus, standing in the aisle. Someone is sure to get off the bus soon, and you will have talent already in place to fill the seat.

Opportunistic hiring comes in different forms. Let's say a talented individual applies for a position in your company. Maybe they aren't a good fit for that particular role, but they would work well elsewhere in the company. If you're opportunistic, you will find a place for that person, even if it means creating an entirely new role.

Another type of opportunistic hiring is to take advantage of changes in your marketplace. For instance, say one of your competitors is going through a buyout or merger. The people in that company are likely feeling uncertain about their futures, and they may begin fleeing the ship like rats. That's an ideal time for you to be opportunistic and pick off the top talent.

For the most effective opportunistic hiring, every single employee in your company should be conscripted into an "active" recruiting role. Every employee should be on the lookout for talent. Assessment and selection is a never-ending battle, and the organizations that understand this stand apart from their competition.

# EVERYONE IS RESPONSIBLE FOR ATTRACTING TALENT

In the Special Operations community, everyone is in charge of talent acquisition and development. It should be the same in the business world. Your CHRO and HR department should drive recruitment, but ultimately, *everyone* is responsible for attracting talent. Everybody from your company is a representation of your brand and your culture, for both good and bad, and everybody is a talent scout.

In the military, the different branches are all targeting the same talent. Green Berets, Navy SEALS, Rangers, MARSOC, and Air Force PJS and Combat Controllers (CCTS) are all competing for the talented individuals who want to be operators. Why would someone choose to be a MARSOC Raider over a Ranger, or a SEAL over an Air Force PJ? Branding plays a role, but the most important differentiator is the people. Mike chose to join the Marine Corps because of Staff Sergeant Ben, a Force Reconnaissance Marine. He later chose to join the Navy SEALS because of the SEALS he worked alongside. Special Operations soldiers are walking advertisements for their particular branches.

*Your employees and alumni are your*
*best advertisement—your greatest*
*weapon in attracting talent.*

Your people are proof that your EVP isn't just words but something you live and breathe. Every company says it wants talent and makes lofty promises to candidates. As Ben Horowitz, famed tech

CEO and venture capitalist, says in his book *What You Do Is Who You Are,* "Who you are is not the values you list on the wall. It's not what you say in a company-wide meeting. It's not your marketing campaign. It's not even what you believe. Who you are is what you do." Your people are the measure of what you actually *do.* They are the experts in what it is like to work at your organization.

If you have talented employees and alumni who take pride in your organization and their work, who live and breathe the core values of your company, then when a potential future employee meets these people, their first inclination will be "I need to become part of that organization." On the other hand, if you have medi-ocre or unhappy employees and alumni, talented candidates will recognize the negativity and look elsewhere. Your current talent is out in the market, just like your product or service. If you say your product or service is the best, your talent should reflect that.

You want your employees and alumni to be like Staff Sergeant Ben. You want talented individuals to take one look and say, "That's who I want to be."

In addition to positively representing your company, your employees can be great talent scouts. The foremost way people find jobs is through employee referrals. Referrals are the most efficient, cost-effective way to hire people. "Always be recruiting" should be the motto.

If you're not leveraging your employees and alumni to attract talent, you're wasting an important resource, but obviously, the person making the recommendation matters. You should place more weight on recommendations from your highest perform-ers, because A-players select other A-players, whereas B-players select B-players and C-players select C-players. In the next chapter, we will discuss the importance of involving A-players in the hiring process.

## KEY TAKEAWAYS

- The key to attracting talent is to market yourself as a talent magnet. As CHRO Don Robertson says, "Great talent is attracted to places that value great talent."
- To show that you value talent, you must provide the things talent wants: competitive pay, talented leaders and colleagues, a sense of community, challenge, growth opportunities, and purpose.
- Your talent marketing strategy should include an employee value proposition (EVP) and social media engagement to effectively tell your story.
- Your current employees and alumni are your best recruiting mechanism.
- Everyone is responsible for talent acquisition. Remember: employee referrals are the number one way people find jobs.

Pararescue Jumper / Combat Rescue Officer (PJ/CRO) Indoctrination Course candidates practice water skills during their extended day of training conducted at Joint Base San Antonio. The PJ/CRO Indoctrination is a nine-week course conducted by the 350th Battlefield Airmen (BA) Training Squadron, BA Training Group, 37th Training Wing, AETC.

*Source: Defense Visual Information Distribution Service / Johnny Saldivar*

# CHAPTER 8

# BUILD YOUR HIRING TEAM: A-PLAYERS SELECT A-PLAYERS

ike every good SEAL, Mike wanted to go to war. Going to war to combat evil is every special operator's ultimate purpose, just like making sales is every salesperson's purpose. Mike had deployed to Iraq three times, first to Baghdad and Ramadi in 2005, then to the Battle of Ramadi in 2006, then to the Battle of Sadr City in 2008. He'd proven himself on the front lines, and at the end of his third deployment, he wanted to take a platoon commander tour, leading twenty SEALS back into either Iraq or Afghanistan. He had more combat experience than most of his peers. But when Mike expressed his desire to become a platoon commander, his senior leaders said no.

To put it mildly, Mike was not pleased. The decision hurt his ego. He knew he could outperform the majority of his peers on the battlefield as a ground force commander, for the simple fact that he had proven so in combat. His skills as a leader had been tested, refined, and strengthened through the Battles of Ramadi and Sadr City, two challenging combat engagements of the Iraq War. A platoon commander position was the natural next step, the place where he could best serve his fellow SEALS and country. Instead, his senior leaders wanted to pull him off the front line and put him behind the scenes, as the director of the SEAL Junior Officer Training Course (JOTC), a one-month leadership development course where recent SEAL officer graduates prepare to become combat leaders.

Orders are orders, and Mike took the job, replacing Leif Babin, coauthor of *Extreme Ownership*, who had held the position since 2006. Mike and Leif Babin were close friends and teammates, having fought in the Battle of Ramadi together, and Mike highly admired how Leif had dramatically transformed the training course, updating it to reflect the modern battlefields of Afghanistan and Iraq. Though Mike could easily recognize how Babin's hard work had impacted the whole of the SEAL organization, Mike couldn't get excited about the role himself.

Once he was thrust into the position, things started to change. As he passed on the lessons he'd learned, the young men in training listened intently to every word, hungry for more. With each day, Mike's sense of impact grew greater. He loved how eager the brand-new SEAL officers were to get out onto the battlefield to lead men, and he felt a responsibility to them. It was his job to prepare them as best as possible. If they failed on the battlefield, it wasn't their fault; it was his. And if he failed, lives were on the line.

Though Mike grew to be deeply invested in his role as trainer, it wasn't until years later, after he'd retired, that he fully understood his level of impact. As the men he mentored headed out to the front lines and advanced in their careers, he started to receive emails thanking him for the lessons he'd bestowed and the wisdom he'd shared. Once these men were on the battlefield, it became clear just how critical the training Mike provided was.

A single individual can accomplish only so much on their own, but when you put a talented individual in charge of selecting and training other talented individuals, their impact grows exponentially. The greatest responsibility of all leaders is to be a coach and mentor and to develop the subordinate leaders below them. The future of every organization relies on *new talent*. True leaders want their organization to accelerate at a greater rate when they leave, and that means selecting and training the best talent.

When you take someone off the front line to help with talent acquisition, it may seem as if you're relegating them to lesser, behind-the-scenes work. But talent is *the* most important factor in your business's success. When you pull your A-players away from their normal duties, you're not putting them behind the scenes; you're putting them on a different kind of front line: the front line of the talent war. They become the gatekeepers for your organization, the ones who will ultimately decide whether you win or fail. To put anyone in this role except for your A-players is foolish at best, and at worst, fatal for your organization.

# CREATING THE HIRING TEAM

Creating the hiring team is one of the most important decisions to make in the talent war, but we see companies make the same four mistakes again and again:

1. B-players or C-players are put in charge of hiring.
2. The hiring team is homogenous.
3. There is no training.
4. Hiring is a secondary function.

### MISTAKE #1: B-PLAYERS OR C-PLAYERS ARE PUT IN CHARGE OF HIRING

The worst mistake you can make with your hiring team is filling it with B- or C-players or whoever happens to be available. The traditional thought is that these are the people who can be spared. Hiring is your front line in the talent war. You don't want people who can be spared; you want the best.

There are three reasons you need A-players in charge of your hiring: (1) talent is attracted to talent, (2) it takes talent to recognize talent, and (3) A-players want other A-players.

"Your assessors have to be the soldier the candidates aspire to be," Brian Decker, former US Army Special Forces Commander for Assessment and Selection, says. "Each assessor is a direct reflection of the regiment." As discussed in the previous chapter, talent is attracted to other talent. The people in charge of hiring are the face of your company. You want them to make a good impression on potential hires.

Brian continues, "My sergeant major picked the best soldiers to be assessors. *It's hard for the regiment to be better than the people selecting the candidates.*" Your A-players are your top talent— your high potentials who have transformed into high performers. They're the people who have proven themselves in the actual function of their job. Your A-players know exactly what it takes to perform to the highest standards, and they will be able to recognize those attributes in others. As CHRO Don Robertson says, "A-talent recognizes and can hire A-talent."

In BUD/S or the Q Course, instructors often ask themselves, "Would I want to deploy with this student?" If the answer is no, then that student is not going to become a SEAL or Green Beret. In a war, you can't settle for mediocrity. It shouldn't be any different in a company. A-players understand this. They recognize that their teammates have a direct impact on the company's bottom line and their own performance. They won't hire subpar talent, because they don't want to work with subpar talent.

In comparison to A-players, B-players and C-players have more difficulty recognizing raw talent. When they do recognize it, they often fear it. Their egos get in the way. They don't want to hire themselves out of a job, so they avoid hiring anyone who is better than them. Instead, they hire other B-players and C-players.

One of the most amazing things about A-players is their ability to check their egos and identify younger candidates who have the potential to become better than them. A-players don't fear other high performers. They like it because it raises their performance as well and creates healthy competition. When Mike was a troop commander, he wanted every soldier below him to overtake him, because

185

that was best for the organization, raising the bar for performance and overall effectiveness. When you can hire someone better than yourself, it means your company is evolving and getting better.

It's also critical to have A-players in HR and talent acquisition, as these people are the first gate for bringing talent into the organization. A-level talent consultants understand the value of talent, know well how to evaluate it, and understand how to align that evaluation with the culture of the firm, as well as the personality and gaps on the team they are hiring for. Great talent consultants are a multiplier of talent, serving as the watchdogs and guardians for all the company's talent needs, so you need A-players in these roles.

## MISTAKE #2: THE HIRING TEAM IS HOMOGENOUS

The hiring team should not be homogenous to the function, meaning if you're hiring for a sales role, the hiring team should be composed of salespeople *and* people from other departments. Talent is talent is talent. Talented A-players can recognize the raw attributes of talent regardless of function. Pick the A-players from any department—manufacturing, engineering, finance, law, etc.—and they will be able to identify and hire talent.

If your hiring team is homogenous, you lose out on diversity of thought. What tends to happen is the team defaults to industry experience or the people that look like them. They look at the university the candidate attended and what companies they previously worked at. In contrast, when your hiring team comes from different functions, talent becomes the focus, because talent is the one thing all the team members share.

Plus, your departments should be working together, so they should be hiring together too. Homogenous hiring teams encourage the creation of silos at work, where each department functions as its own entity, without connecting to the larger team. Some of the most successful companies—like Amazon, for instance—specifically involve A-players from other departments in the hiring process to help eliminate silo bias.

## MISTAKE #3: THERE IS NO TRAINING

The skills of talent assessment and selection are not innate. In the military, there are a multitude of procedures and processes to put someone in an instructor role. There are courses and instructors for the instructors. There is *training*.

In the corporate world, George has been deeply disappointed by the lack of training and enforcement of procedures related to talent acquisition. The hiring process typically varies widely from hiring manager to hiring manager, resulting in inconsistent talent in the organization. Interviewers often ask irrelevant questions or, worse, questions that could result in litigation. They sometimes give a candidate top scores simply because they like or know the candidate, or they mistakenly hire a candidate with the wrong set of strengths, like a highly detail-oriented person for a role that requires creative, free-form thinking.

If you want your hiring team to hire the best talent, you need to set them up for success. That means training them. Putting an untrained hiring team in front of a candidate is like putting an untrained person behind a gun. It won't end well. Don't assume people know how to interview for talent. Even if they've been trained at a previous organization, nobody should interview until they've been through *your* interviewing training. You also can't assume that your hiring team will pick up a talent mindset by osmosis. Training is a far more effective way for you to instill a talent mindset. If you train your hiring team how to effectively interview and assess for *talent*, they are more likely to identify talented candidates.

This is also your opportunity to assess whether the members of your hiring team have the maturity and capacity to be charged with selecting your next generation of employees and leaders. Not all SEALS or Green Berets initially assigned to assessment and selection complete the training to become a BUD/S or Q Course instructor. It is a privilege and honor to become a gatekeeper into your community, much like the title hiring manager.

Part of training is communicating what the company needs in the new hire. The hiring team needs to be on the same page as upper-level leadership when it comes to succession planning, and they should work in partnership with HR to ensure they are in sync with the organization's overall talent strategy. They also need to have a forward-focused view of the organization. Don Robertson says, "The person doing the selection has to be cognizant of the types of things that the company's going to be facing in the future." The hiring team needs this awareness so that they can hire not for what the company needs today but what it will need three, five, or ten years down the line.

Some companies do offer training in interviewing and hiring, but it is often optional or limited to the basics. In the military, SOF instructors continually consult with their counterparts returning from the front line regarding the efficacy of the training programs. If soldiers are meeting something on the battlefield that they weren't trained for, then the training must change. You need a similar feedback loop in your company. If your hiring teams are not hiring talent, you need to reassess your training.

## MISTAKE #4: HIRING IS A SECONDARY FUNCTION

To hire talent, you need a dedicated hiring team, but the majority of companies treat hiring as a secondary function. An administrative HR employee is told to screen job candidates on top of their normal workload. A salesperson is told to clear a day on their calendar to interview candidates. A hiring manager splits their attention once or twice a year to hire a new team member.

People can only perform their primary duty the best. Everything else will receive half effort. It's human nature. Salespeople's primary function is sales. They are focused on one thing and one thing only: generating as many sales and as much revenue as possible. Their paychecks and performance metrics are all tied to that primary mission, so they will prioritize it over a secondary mission of recruitment.

In Special Operations, the instructors in charge of training are taken "off-line," meaning they are pulled from the front lines so they can focus exclusively on training. They aren't going to war *and* training people. They're just *training* people. If their attention was split between battle and training, they would not be able to perform either function to the needed standard. A common mantra in the Special Operations community is "Two things shitty, and one thing well." If you want your hiring team to be most effective, they need to focus solely on talent acquisition. It needs to be their full-time job.

This may sound like an impossible suggestion. You might be thinking, "We can't waste so many resources on a non-revenue-generating function!" Remember, though, that the hiring process is actually your *largest* revenue generator in the long term. It is your people who generate revenue, and the hiring process is what gets you the best people, who will generate the most revenue.

Ideally, within your HR department, you will have at least one dedicated recruiter, whose only function is recruitment. This person will be the first gatekeeper. Their job is to recruit passive candidates and screen active candidates.

Next, in an optimal situation, we recommend creating six-month rotational acquisition roles. These roles are to be filled by A-players, from a variety of departments, as chosen by each department's manager. For example, the sales leader will choose the best salesperson to shift their primary function from sales to talent acquisition. For six months, this salesperson will focus exclusively on funneling talent into the organization. Yes, we are telling you to take your best salesperson off-line and put them in charge of hiring your next generation of salespeople. It may hurt in the short-term, but it will accelerate you in the long-term. Someone who hires only one or two people every couple of years is ill-equipped to be a professional assessor and selector of talent. In contrast, someone who is completely dedicated to hiring for six months is far better equipped.

This rotational team of A-players forms the second and most intensive gate into the organization. Any candidate who makes it through this gate should have the raw attributes you have identified as part of the talent profile for the role, as discussed in chapter 6, "Know Thyself."

The final gate is the hiring manager and, in some cases, any appropriate C-suite leaders or senior executives. At this gate, the hiring function should be secondary and not primary. Your leaders must remain dedicated to their primary mission and cannot take six months off for talent acquisition, and they don't need to, because the A-player gate has already effectively assessed and filtered the talent. They simply need to offer their stamp of approval.

The three gatekeeper layers we recommend represent an *ideal* situation. Ultimately, though, hiring is a demand-based business. The military has a constant demand, which supports the practice of taking A-players off-line for talent assessment and selection. Larger firms may also have a constant demand, but small- to medium-sized businesses often do not. Scale these recommendations in accordance with your level of hiring. If you only need to hire a handful of new employees in a year, it is not practical to create a primary function for hiring. The demand simply isn't there. This does not alleviate you from training your staff as future hiring managers. Remember—it's a mindset you are creating!

However, the larger your company, the more important it is to create primary hiring functions. As companies grow, they tend to shift to a butts-in-seats mentality, which dilutes the quality of their talent and their culture. If you are in the midst of massive growth, you are setting yourself up for failure if you don't apply these principles. You need to put your A-players in charge to ensure you are building the right infrastructure of people to support your growth.

Taking your A-players off-line won't be easy. The military has a plug-and-play structure. For any given role, there are multiple qualified individuals to fill it, because the military has created world-class talent acquisition and development programs. This allows the leadership to move people wherever they are most effective, like taking someone off-line to fill a training role. In civilian organizations, people's work is often structured in a way that they are "irreplaceable." As we discussed in chapter 6, "Know Thyself," you ideally should never be in a position where the loss of a single person creates a vacuum in your organization. We understand, though, that companies don't always operate under ideal circumstances. Taking your A-players off-line may require sacrifice. For instance, your top salespeople likely have unique relationships with clients. To rotate them out, you must create a transition process to transfer those clients to other salespeople. Yes, it's more work, but the impact can be transformative for your organization.

When you take your A-players off-line, you are operating from a strategic mindset instead of a tactical mindset. As CEO Joe DePinto says, "You're thinking not only of the short, intermediate terms but the long term of how critical it is to find great talent." Many companies today have a short-term view, where they're worried about meeting metrics for the quarter or what stockholders will think. This is a tactical mindset. Great organizations that continue to grow and thrive have a long-term strategic mindset.

## INCENTIVIZING YOUR A-PLAYERS TO JOIN THE HIRING TEAM

Whether in business or on the battlefield, A-players want to be in the game. They may not want to take a hiring role, so you must provide them with incentives to do so.

First and foremost, you must communicate *why* hiring is so important. Unless you already have a firmly established talent mindset at your company, your A-players might see the switch to hiring as a demotion, because they don't understand the value of talent acquisition. You must convey that value. Fortunately, most A-players have a strong sense of collectivism. If they believe that working on the hiring team is what's best for the organization, then that's what they will do.

You can't rely on altruistic goodwill alone. You must also offer adequate financial compensation. Under no circumstances should you force your A-players to take a pay cut to join the hiring team. They should be paid the same (or more) than what they would earn in their normal role.

Additionally, serving on the hiring team must be seen as both personally and professionally enhancing. You must communicate to your A-players that participating in assessment and selection will afford them exponential impact within the organization and a clear reward in terms of professional development. The assessment and selection of talent is an integral skill of leadership. An effective leader should be able to shift between every function within your company, from operations to training to hiring. As such, serving on the hiring team should be a required step to moving up in your organization. It should be something your

A-players *want* to do because they know it's how they will get to the next level.

Demand and ensure you have A-players on the front lines of the talent war with you. Always.

Once you've selected a hiring team, the next step is the hiring process itself. In the next chapter, we will detail strategies and best practices for an effective hiring process.

## KEY TAKEAWAYS

- A-players hire A-players.
- Your hiring team should not be homogenous.
- You must train your hiring team.
- Hiring is most effective when it is a primary, not secondary, function.
- To incentivize your A-players to take on hiring functions, link talent acquisition to job.

# PART III

# GOING TO WAR

US Army Rangers, assigned to 2nd Battalion, 75th Ranger Regiment, prepare for extraction from their objective during Task Force Training on Fort Hunter Liggett, California. To earn the right to don the tan beret and become a member of the 75th Ranger Regiment, candidates must undergo Ranger Assessment and Selection (RASP), an intense eight-week course designed to test a soldier's physical and mental strength under extreme conditions.

*Source: Defense Visual Information Distribution Service / Spc. Steven Hitchcock*

# CHAPTER 9

# THE HIRING PROCESS: A DECISIVE BATTLEFIELD

In the previous chapters, we covered the prep work that leads up to hiring. It starts with a talent mindset—a deep belief in the power of talent—and a commitment to hiring for character and training for skill. You then assess your top performers and conduct succession and workforce planning to know what you're looking for. After that, you can build a marketing strategy to attract talent and create a hiring team of your A-players. Finally, you are ready for the actual assessment and selection process.

In Special Operations, assessment and selection is unique in that it is combined with training. It has been proven that this approach works, building Special Operations into one of the most effective and agile organizations in the world. While no business can—or should—perfectly replicate sof selection processes, you can adopt some of the fundamental principles behind the practices.

The Special Forces Assessment and Selection (sfas) and the Special Forces Qualification Course (Q Course)—the assessment, selection, and training pipeline for the Army's Green Berets—provide an excellent roadmap of assessment and selection strategies that businesses can mimic. In the summer of 2010, Brian Decker assumed the role of commander for sfas. He helped to revamp sfas and shared his findings with us.

sfas is set up as a series of test gates. Week one, the selection is all objective. It's intelligence testing, psychological testing, and physical testing, measuring the three separate but important parts of the person as defined in the Whole Man concept: mental, emotional, and physical. There is a checklist of minimum requirements each candidate must meet. For instance, if a candidate's IQ is below 105, they are not selected. Once a candidate passes the minimum requirements, the first gate is closed. All that information is archived, and the candidates start the next week with a clean slate.

Week two is designed to answer the question, "Can we train you?" The instructors put the students through land navigation training to see if they can apply what they learn. After passing that test, the second gate is closed just like the first, and the candidates start the third week fresh. At this point, an initial class of four hundred will have been whittled down to just two hundred.

The third week—"team week"—is when the selection process really begins, in Brian's mind. During team week, the instructors begin searching for the Army Special Operations Forces (arsof) attributes, the eight "Whole Man" traits: perseverance, team player, adaptability, personal responsibility, integrity, courage, profession-alism, and capability. As mentioned in chapter 6, "Know Thyself," searching for numerous attributes at the same time is simply not feasible, so the SFAS instructors focus on just four: perseverance, team player, adaptability, and personal responsibility. "The attributes became the conceptual framework or competency model that we measured all subjective data collection against," Brian explained.

"We defined those attributes in a behavioral manner," said Brian, "because we can't measure an attribute, but if we can identify the behaviors associated with an attribute, that is a good approximate measure." They then created a "behaviorally anchored rating system" (sometimes called a BARS) with scores from one to five. The instructor cadre was trained on how to assign ratings and went through inter-rater reliability testing so that everyone was rating properly, ensuring quality data.

With this new rating system, Brian and his team redesigned every event of team week. Instead of it being about accomplishing the event, it was about how the team responded to various challenges. "We graded the behaviors, or inputs, versus the outcomes of the events," Brian said.

The instructors used predetermined scenarios that included sudden changes to the team's mission. It was *pressure testing*, designed to replicate the complex environment the students would need to operate in as Green Berets. In this VUCA (volatility, uncertainty, complexity, and ambiguity) environment of controlled chaos, the students' true character was revealed.

As the US Army Special Forces Commander for Assessment and Selection, Brian worked to refine SFAS so that it was assessing and selecting attributes that would predict future success as Green Berets. Today, he is applying what he learned about assessing, selecting, and developing talent to the NFL. He teaches talent scouts how to gather better talent using a model of character that he feels predicts success in the NFL. He also works as a mentor, partnering with players to help them grow and develop. Through this work, he has proved that the principles that work for the Green Berets also work in the NFL, and they can benefit your organization too. Specifically, two lessons to take away from SFAS are the importance of *gates* in the hiring process and the need for *pressure testing*.

## A SERIES OF GATES

At each stage of the hiring process, candidates should pass through a gate. Each time, the gate closes, and the information used for that gate does not impact scores in the next gate. The assessment process starts fresh with each new gate, getting more and more refined, zeroing in on those all-important indicators of talent: drive, resiliency, adaptability, humility, integrity, effective intelligence, team-ability, curiosity, and emotional strength. (Remember: you can only look for so many attributes at one time; the specific attributes you look for will vary, depending on your industry, company, and the role.)

The first gate should be a minimum-requirements screening. It will save you and your candidates time and energy. Due to the ease with which people can apply for jobs online, a single position can attract an unmanageable number of applicants. The best way to deal with the bulk of applicants is to use "knockout questions" to filter out the clearly unqualified candidates—the candidates who do not meet the minimum requirements for hard skills, experience, or education.

Initial screening is necessary, but be careful with your knockout questions. Your screening criteria *must* make sense for the role. Brian Decker said of his time in SFAS, "I tried to not allow something that's not predictive of success to cause attrition." Your minimum requirements should be the *true* qualifications needed for succeeding in the role.

Once the minimum requirements are met, the gate closes, and you stop looking at basic requirements and start focusing on assessing *character*. There are three major strategies you can use at this gate: interviewing, observing candidates in action, and administering assessment tests. For the highest quality information, this gate should be a *multivariate* process, meaning at least two of these strategies should be used. It should also contain both subjective and objective assessments. As Brian says, assessment and selection are "a mix of art and science."

The exact process and assessment techniques you use will depend on the role. You're not going to put an entry-level employee through multiple rounds of full-day interviews, and you're not going to put a director through an entry-level computer coding test. Every role has its own requirements. You should adapt the process based on the role's impact on the organization as well as the role's talent profile.

Regardless of role, if you want to reveal a person's character, it's important to pressure test them, because character is revealed at one's limits.

## CHARACTER IS REVEALED AT ONE'S LIMITS

Everyone can put on a good-looking facade when things are easy, but who cares how people act when they win? What happens when things don't work out the way they expect?

Under pressure, an individual's true behavior comes out. Adversity doesn't just build character; it reveals it. "The real 'us' shows up when things get tough and challenging and gritty," says retired Navy SEAL Commander Rich Diviney. "When we're under stress, we start defaulting. Skills begin to degrade, and we have to lean on our character attributes instead."

There are different ways to pressure test. In the Q Course, they sought to increase uncertainty by challenging the students with problems that did not always have clear solutions. "The solution to any problem is typically seen as stability," Brian says. "Once candidates stabilize and solve a problem, there's not a lot to observe. It's only during those periods of time when they're assessing the problem and searching for a solution that you truly see the talent displayed. So we made the environment complex. We made it uncertain. We made it difficult."

In BUD/S, the instructors use physical challenges to push students to the limit. "The process strips you down to the raw basics," Rich explains, "and asks the question, 'Do you have what it takes?'" The human body is incredibly resilient, so the mind will break before the body. As such, though the BUD/S challenges are physical, they are intended to reveal students' character—their drive and resiliency. As Brian says, "Desire is the most fundamental demand placed on high achievement. You can't coach it, so you better have a selection process that has a mountain in the middle of it." A pressure test can be that mountain, as Mike learned firsthand.

## MIKE FEELS THE PRESSURE

*This is it,* Mike thought, staring up at the rope. *I'm going to fail out of* BUD/S. *Because of a freaking rope.*

Two weeks prior, Mike had completed Hell Week. The instructors had even pulled him aside and told him, "You're one of the standout leaders in this class. We know what you can do as a leader, so we need you to step aside so that we can test and evaluate the other officers."

Yet now, Mike was struggling to climb a basic rope like he had been climbing since day one of the Marine Corps. He'd been climbing ropes for *years*, and he was good at it. He'd never failed to get up one, until now.

For the first time in training, Mike was displaying serious signs of fatigue. It was an ideal moment to test him, so the instructors dug in, shouting up at him. The other students, who had already completed the exercise, watched from their nearby formation. Mike started up the rope again. He could sense all the eyes on him, could feel the pressure. He made it ten feet and dropped. The instructors kept yelling, and Mike started up the rope again. And again. And again.

Mike was frustrated. He felt like a dirtbag for not being able to get up the rope, but there was no way he was going to quit. He started up the rope again. And fell again. He got to his feet and prepared to start up the rope again, but the instructors stopped him and pulled him aside, out of view from the other students.

"It's okay. We all have these days," one of the instructors said. "We wanted to apply some pressure to see how you would react and whether you would quit."

The instructors didn't really care whether Mike made it to the top of the rope or not. "The beauty of BUD/S," says retired SEAL Master Chief Jason Tuschen, "is it finds your Achilles' heel, whether it's in Hell Week or the first phase, or mine happened to be pool week [dive competency testing], and I was an experienced swimmer. That, to me, was such a mental hurdle to overcome."

The rope wasn't Mike's biggest Achilles' heel during the one year of SEAL training, but on that specific day, it was his biggest mental hurdle, and overcoming mental hurdles is the point of BUD/S training. SEAL training is difficult for everyone, but for some, it's easier. Those are the people who especially need to be tested. So as soon as the instructors saw their opportunity, they ratcheted up the pressure to see if Mike would cave, and in this case, he didn't. While he may have failed at the rope, he passed the much more important test in the eyes of the instructors—the test of drive and resiliency.

Obviously, companies are not going to put job candidates through an intensive, physically challenging six-month training program like BUD/S. As Rich says, "You can't take a business team and throw them in the surf zone for thirty minutes because (a) it's not going to be legal, and (b) it's not applicable to the business environment." Though the tactics you use will be different, the strategy is the same. You simply need to tailor the pressure testing to the situation.

## TAILOR THE TEST TO THE SITUATION

For pressure testing to be effective, the environment must replicate the job reality. If you want to see how someone will perform on the job, then testing conditions should reflect true conditions, especially worst-case scenarios.

When Brian first took command of SFAS, the test conditions did not match the job. "The intersection of complexity and instability is where SOF operates and thrives," he said, "but the assessment environment was anything but that. It was simple, it was stable. It was the equivalent of training you to accomplish a task in the day but testing you in the dark." Because the environment did not reflect the Green Berets' operational environment, a lot of information they were using to assess and select candidates was flawed. Rather than identifying people who would make good Green Berets, they were only identifying people who made good Q Course students.

This is a common problem in hiring. People all too often hire someone who can write a great resume and interview well. That's not the same thing as someone who will be great on the job.

An office environment is vastly different from a Special Operations environment, so obviously, your pressure tests will look different. You can create pressure in a variety of ways. You could introduce time constraints, or you could put a candidate into a scenario where they have to work with others to solve a problem. You could have them complete a work sample or give a presentation to a large group of people. It could even be as simple as having a board of interviewers ask challenging, scenario-based questions.

The important thing is that the test reflects actual working conditions as much as is reasonable. If a candidate will be working in an environment requiring fast, on-the-spot thinking and action, then introducing time constraints is justified. If, however, you are hiring for a creative role that requires thoughtful planning, then time constraints would do more harm than good.

In Special Operations, pressure testing typically takes place in a training environment; in business, the best place to introduce pressure testing is in interviews.

## INTERVIEWS

Interviews are perhaps the most critical battlefield in the hiring process. In *Powerful*, Patty McCord emphasized the importance of interviews, which were a top priority at Netflix: "Interviews trumped any meeting a hiring manager was scheduled for and they were the only reason that attendees of our executive staff could miss a meeting or leave early."[19] The effectiveness of your interview process will have a direct impact on the quality of your new hires.

The exact interview procedure will vary according to role. For instance, lower-level roles may require a single interview, while higher-level leadership roles need several interviews. As a general rule, don't put candidates through more interviews than you really need. And if you are putting a candidate through multiple interviews, consider varying the type of interview, including both

---

19  Patty McCord, *Powerful: Building a Culture of Freedom and Responsibility* (Silicon Guild, 2018), 103.

one-on-one interviews (one interviewer and one candidate) and panel interviews (two to four interviewers and one candidate).

Though the procedure may vary, the strategy behind the interviews should be similar. For guidance on strategy, look to Special Operations murder boards. Murder boards are not quite as terrifying as they sound. They are full of pressure but professionally run. An operator sits on one side of the table, and on the other is a psychologist and five to eight senior enlisted and officers representing the entire community. The psychologist has previously assessed the operator to identify potential red flags. The senior panel then digs in, raising the pressure by probing the red flags and presenting complex scenarios. They ask difficult questions and push against sore spots to see how the operator reacts.

If you approach your interviews a little more like SOF murder boards, you can reveal valuable information. To that end, we have five tips:

1. Know what you're looking for with each question.
2. Create a core set of questions to be used with each candidate.
3. Ask scenario-based and behavioral questions.
4. Add challenges.
5. Push candidates outside their comfort zone.

## KNOW WHAT YOU'RE LOOKING FOR

You need to know what you're looking for with each question. "When I interview somebody," says Don Robertson, "I am clear on what outcomes I want, and I ask about experiences that demonstrate to me that a candidate can deliver those outcomes." In chapter 6, "Know Thyself," we talked about identifying the attributes of your top performers. Those attributes are what will lead you to the outcomes you want. Your questions should be designed to elicit information about certain behaviors so that you can measure the attributes identified in the relevant talent profile, like drive or humility.

As Brian discovered in Green Beret assessment and selection, you can only focus on so many behaviors and attributes at one time. Interviewing is difficult. If your interviewers are trying to assess multiple traits with each question, they'll be overwhelmed and will not rate candidates as accurately. Instead, link each question to a single behavior or attribute. For instance, one question might be designed to reveal a candidate's adaptability. Since you're not measuring humility with that question, you shouldn't be scoring for it; you should only score adaptability. Later, a different question can be used to assess humility.

As mentioned in the previous chapter, your hiring team needs to be trained in interviewing. If they're not taught what a good answer looks like, they won't be able to recognize it. You should provide an "answer sheet," with examples of the types of answers—both good and bad—that interviewers should look for. If there aren't clear guidelines about what a question is intended to reveal, then by default, interviewers will score based on their gut, allowing more personal bias into the process. Also be thoughtful about which interviewers ask which questions. If a question is meant to reveal information about a candidate's team-ability, then the person asking the question should have high levels of team-ability themselves.

Once you know what you're looking for with each question, the next step is to create a set of core, standardized questions that will be asked of each candidate.

## STANDARDIZED QUESTIONS

SOF assessment is repeatable and standardized. Yes, there is constant iteration and improvement, like Brian's changes to SFAS, but for the most part, the process remains the same. This is critical for two reasons. First, the standardization allows for a robust feedback loop. Since the processes are the same for each candidate, it is easy to go back and review their effectiveness. Second, it ensures a consistent level of quality. From one year to the next, the people who make it through SOF assessment and selection are of the same caliber. As General William Boykin says, "I walked [the assessment and selection course for the highly selective and specialized Army Special Operations unit] forty years ago, but I know that the young man today is walking the same terrain and meeting the same standards because the standards haven't changed. How the course is run has changed with technology and improvements, but the standards have not."

Research has shown that having a structured, standardized set of interview questions is one of the best ways to make your screening process more effective.[20] CHRO Tom Lokar says, "If there's one thing I'd recommend to everyone, it is some sort of structured interview."

20 "Effective Interviews," Society for Industrial and Organizational Psychology, accessed January 3, 2020, https://www.siop.org/Business-Resources/ Employment-Testing/Effective-Interviews.

If you don't have a core set of standardized questions, there is no way for you to properly compare candidates. You want to compare apples to apples, not apples to oranges. Additionally, if you're using different questions for each candidate, you are not treating everyone fairly, and it will be difficult to build a solid feedback loop. Let's say you hire five people, and three of them go on to be top performers. When you look back at your hiring process to figure out where you went right and wrong, you won't be able to find any patterns, because each person went through a different process.

For this reason, at least a portion of the interview should be structured such that the same questions are asked of every candidate. A well-designed, standardized, repeatable core set of questions with a good answer sheet is the anchor for your interviews. But not all questions are created equal; scenario-based and behavioral questions are best.

## SCENARIO-BASED AND BEHAVIORAL QUESTIONS

In murder boards, the interviews are weighted heavily toward scenario-based and behavioral questions, as these questions have been shown to work better than most other forms of questions. A scenario-based question involves asking the candidate about how they would handle a hypothetical situation—"Given this scenario, what would you do?" A behavioral question is one that asks about how they handled a past experience—"Tell me about a time you did x."

These types of questions are ideal because they reveal the candidate's thought process and behaviors. The answer itself is important, but also important is *how* the candidate reaches the answer.

How genuine are they in their response? How do they approach the problem? What is their decision-making process? In the solution, do they involve other people or do it all themselves? For scenario-based questions, remember to replicate the job environment. Give them a real-life scenario from your company and have them walk you through how they would handle it.

Scenario-based and behavioral questions are excellent for assessing a person's key attributes, especially resiliency. CHRO Tracy Keogh stressed the importance of asking about candidates' experiences with failure to learn about their resiliency.

"I always ask people to tell me about a time they failed and how they dealt with it," says Tracy. She says there are three types of answers, and each one reveals important information. "First, you get the people who can't come up with any time they ever failed. Either they aren't being truthful, or they haven't done anything interesting and are not taking any risks. The next set of people tell you about a failure, but they clearly didn't learn anything from it and didn't overcome it. The final group tells you about a failure, what they did to overcome it, what lessons they took from it, and how they improved moving forward. These are the people we're most interested in."

Another way to assess candidates' resiliency and other core attributes is to give them challenges to overcome in the interview.

## CHALLENGES

Incorporating challenges into the interview process is a great way to see candidates in action. Challenges are exercises where the candidate must *do* something. Challenges should reflect the duties of the job. Tom Lokar calls these challenges "realistic job preview gates that allow you to see the person in action and to understand what they bring that's going to be immediately beneficial to the company."

Challenges come in a wide range. You may ask a candidate to prepare a writing sample or to give a presentation on a topic they're unfamiliar with. One of the most well-known challenges for salespeople is to hand them an object—like a pen—and ask them to sell it to you. These challenges give you a sneak peek at how the candidate would perform in the role.

One of the best types of challenge is a *case study*. These are standardized written fictional scenarios that range in complexity, depending on how much time you want to give to the candidate. If the candidate has fifteen minutes of prep time, the case study should be short. If they have a week's notice, then the case study will probably be several pages long and include charts and data and will require a twenty-minute or more presentation on the day of the final round of interviews.

Special Operations employs this same case study methodology in assessment and selection for future Special Operations officers. The prospective officers are given a robust target intelligence package (which contains the necessary information for mission planning and preparation to conduct a real-world operation) and told to plan a mission in a short period of time, ranging from thirty minutes to two hours. This is often called a "sand table" drill in the military.

The assessors are looking for how the prospective officers make use of their time, what critical information they utilize from the target intelligence package, and what additional questions they ask, given intentional gaps in the instructions and target intelligence package. The assessors are primarily interested in the prospective officers' thought processes, the way they deal with the time-constraint stress, and their ability to clearly, concisely, and confidently communicate a simple plan. What matters the least during this process is that their plan is actually tactically (technically) sound. The assessors can teach the prospective officers the technical aspects to create a sound tactical plan once they pass the assessment and selection.

## PUSHING CANDIDATES OUTSIDE THEIR COMFORT ZONE

People feel stable and safe when they immediately know the answer to a question. Remember: stressors reveal the truth of a person's character. To create some pressure, ask questions where the "right" answer is not immediately apparent.

There are several good reasons to push candidates outside their comfort zone. If they will be working in an environment that requires them to be cool, calm, and collected, which is every environment, whether at war or in business, then you need to make sure that they don't get flustered by the unknown and uncomfortable. Candidates—good ones, at least—will prepare answers ahead of time for traditional interview questions. By asking them unexpected questions, you knock them off balance and force them to think about something other than what they came to do, which is sell themselves by demonstrating an expert understanding of both their strengths and weaknesses.

George makes good use of this technique when he's interviewing candidates, especially for senior-level roles. Some of his favorite questions are: How confident are you in your ability to lead and achieve in this role if you can't make any changes to the people on the team? Who would you hire for this role other than yourself, and why? If you were to gather your best friends—the ones you'd trust to erase your phone in the event of your demise—what would that group unanimously say is their pet peeve about you? These questions allow him to assess how a candidate operates under stress, as well as evaluate their authenticity and integrity.

Another method is to delve into any red flags the candidate has shown. People typically don't like talking about their weak areas, but it's a great way to gain insight into their character. As we discussed earlier, you don't want to screen too heavily based on red flags, because everyone has them, but you *do* want to investigate them. There's a twofold benefit here: you determine the strength and validity of any red flags, and you see how the candidate acts under pressure.

By following our five tips, your interview process will be better designed to assess and select for talent as opposed to hard skills. On top of interviews, one of the best ways to assess candidates is to observe them in action.

## OUR LEAST FAVORITE INTERVIEW QUESTION

"Why should we hire you?" We *dislike* this question. First, it encourages ingratiating answers, where the candidate says what they think you want to hear. Second, the applicant will always get this question wrong, because no candidate is going to know your company like you do. It's not their job to know why you should hire them; that's *your* job.

When George gives advice to people interviewing, he says, "Ultimately, it's not what you know about the company; it's how much you know about yourself and whether you can articulate that in a crisp, impactful way."

As an interviewer, yes, you want candidates to do some research into the company. It demonstrates their level of interest in the role. But you can't expect candidates to know what you're looking for. Instead, you want them to focus on what they know about themselves. You gather all that information and make the decision for yourself whether they are a good fit for your company.

## OBSERVING CANDIDATES IN ACTION

Identifying character attributes like resiliency, integrity, and effective intelligence is difficult because you can't see character. You can, however, observe behaviors, which are ultimately driven by character and mindset.

When in action, candidates put their behaviors on display. This allows you to infer the attributes beneath the surface, and it gives you an idea of how they will perform in the role. To see candidates in action, there are two main strategies you can use: role-play exercises and covert observation.

## ROLE PLAY

A great way to see candidates in action is to put them through role-play exercises in which they must act out various job-relevant scenarios. Role-play exercises are a fundamental part of Special Operations assessment, selection, and training. Military psychologist Carroll Greene was involved with the assessment of operators, and he explained, "We would put candidates under high-stress simulations with an ethical and operational dilemma. We could see things in these scenarios that we couldn't see from psychological tests, from background checks, or from interview questioning. A candidate's score in these ethically and operationally complex dilemmas was an excellent predictor of success and performance in the future."

In Special Operations assessment and selection, candidates are put through the same kinds of scenarios they will face as a SEAL, Green Beret, or MARSOC Raider. To replicate battlefield conditions in Afghanistan, instructors might assume the role of a tribal or village elder upset by a recent US Forces raid in his village. The students would be tasked with de-escalating the situation while trying to build rapport with the village elder.

Role-play exercises are powerful because they allow you to see what candidates actually *do* in a given situation, not just what they say they do. Role-play can make you look twice at a candidate you previously overlooked, or it can bring your attention to red flags you missed in an otherwise solid applicant.

The key to making role-play exercises effective is replicating the job environment. For instance, say you have a candidate applying to be a branch manager at a bank. Their role-play exercise should essentially be running a branch for the day, solving various problems that arise. Perhaps there are accounting irregularities, an employee who is thinking about quitting, an upset customer, or new software upgrades that seem to be doing more harm than good.

Role-play is a perfect technique to apply pressure and get an idea of how a candidate would perform in the role. It's also wise to see how a candidate acts when they think no one is watching, which is where covert observation comes in.

---

### ASSESSING ADAPTABILITY: LACK OF STRUCTURE IN SOF TRAINING

When General William Boykin first became involved in the assessment and selection process for a highly selective and specialized Army Special Operations unit, the people he thought would be most successful were often the ones who failed to graduate. He soon discovered the reason. "It came down to structure, or a lack of structure," he told us. "There are people who need absolute structure in their lives to thrive. Part of that structure is you get a manual on everything...Most importantly, you know what standards you have to meet. Well, what happens when you don't know what those standards are?"

Many parts of the military are set up to provide structure, but Special Operations Forces are different. "A lot of these guys [including Green Berets and Rangers] had been around for a long time and had great reputations," General Boykin said. "But now nobody was telling them what the standard was. We simply told them to do the very best they could, and if they didn't meet the standard, we'd let them know. They could not deal with that. Then you had other guys who came out of nowhere, who could deal with the lack of standards because they had been creating a personal structure for themselves in structureless environments all their lives."

The instructors purposefully created a lack of structure because that is the type of environment SOF soldiers operate in. "If we send you out alone," General Boykin explained, "how do we know that you're going to give it your very best, when you've demonstrated to us here that, without knowing what the standard is, you can't give your very best? We want you to go hard. We want you to give it all you got." The instructors didn't want candidates who could strive for and meet a set goal; they wanted candidates who could push themselves past limits, who would do their very best, leaving nothing on the table.

General Boykin and the other instructors were essentially looking for adaptability—people who could function in any situation, even without structure. To find adaptability, they put students into a VUCA (volatility, uncertainty, complexity, and ambiguity) environment, which is the very definition of the business environment. To create a VUCA environment, they withheld many details about training activities.

"There was no structure," General Boykin explained. "The only thing they knew was 'Tomorrow morning we're going to wake you up at five. Have a rucksack that weighs this amount and have these things at a minimum in that rucksack.' That's all. Where are we going? How long are we going to be out? How many tasks? You don't know any of that, nothing. It plays on the minds of those people who have to have structure created for them, who have to know the answers up front."

When people are put into a VUCA environment, General Boykin explained, "they either thrive on it, because they can use their own creative skills to figure it out, or they walk away from it, because it doesn't make sense to them and they can't adapt to it. We chose the people who thrive on it, and that's why we got the best, most capable people."

In business, you need people who can adapt and perform in a VUCA environment. A great strategy to identify those individuals is to remove some structure, as they do in SOF assessment and selection. Give the candidate limited instructions and see how they react—for instance, give them a pitch deck and simply ask, "What do you think?" Or ask scenario-based questions with ambiguous or extraneous information, where it's unclear what you're looking for, and see how they handle it.

Only bring adaptability into your selection strategy for roles where it makes sense. If a candidate is going to be working in a very structured environment, then you don't want to select someone who thrives without structure. For example, General Boykin explained that some of the best soldiers from this highly selective and specialized Army Special Operations unit would not have done as well in a conventional unit: "Some of these people may not have been superstars in a conventional unit, because they were always trying to figure out another way, a different way, a better way. The answer that they always got back was 'We've already tried that—it doesn't work' or 'If it ain't broke, don't fix it.'" If there are roles within your company where proactive problem-solving and idea exploration are discouraged, then the hiring process should reflect a more structured environment.

## COVERT OBSERVATION OF CANDIDATES

The second a candidate walks into your company, every person that interacts with them should be evaluating their behaviors and noting observations. Obviously, you should not cross any ethical lines. When we say "covert" observation, we don't mean that you should spy on your candidates; we mean that you should pay attention to how they act when they believe they're not being assessed. People are on their best behavior during interviews and official assessments. By paying attention to the moments in between, you can see how they act under more normal circumstances.

George went through this kind of covert observation when he was interviewing at a major tech company. An employee—who was not involved in the interview and who was not part of the department George was applying for—was assigned to escort George to the cafeteria and show him the different facilities. The employee was very casual, but she was, in fact, assessing George the whole time. She started with small talk—about where he'd grown up and his family—and eventually keyed in on his current employer, asking what he did and didn't like and what the scope of his work was. Essentially, she wisely knew that you can gain a lot of information about a candidate from a simple conversation. George, being in talent acquisition, was familiar with this kind of covert observation, since he used it himself, but most candidates are unfamiliar with the tactic. Especially after the high-stress situation of an interview, people let their guard down. That's when you can truly observe natural behaviors.

The third and final major strategy of assessing candidates is using assessment tests.

## MAKING USE OF EXTERNAL REFERENCES

Common perception is that reference checks are dead. Negative. They are still alive and kicking—most people simply don't utilize them to their full advantage. References are about reputation, and reputation is everything. In the Special Operations community, it's impossible to advance if you don't have a solid reputation.

External references can give you an insider's look into a candidate, but there are three main challenges with references: (1) They skew positive. (2) They are time-consuming. (3) Fears of legal action can limit the provided information.

Candidates wisely provide references who will say favorable things. To get a more balanced picture of a candidate, you need to dig deeper. Ask questions that challenge the reference to discuss more than the positive. For example, "If you had to pick two areas where this person could improve, what would they be?" If none of a candidate's references are willing to speak openly and honestly, it should raise a red flag, and you should investigate further.

One of the main reasons many companies skip reference checks is time. If you hire five hundred people in a year, that's a lot of phone calls to make for reference checks. For entry-level jobs, you can skip the references, but for leadership roles and positions of high trust, references are necessary. You don't need to reference-check every single candidate, but you must check references for the finalist before making an offer. Spending this extra time to ensure a good hire will save you time and money in the long run.

The final challenge of references is that companies don't want to be sued for what they say. At many companies, the policy for reference checks is to simply confirm whether the candidate worked there. That's the minimum they are required to do, and it is the safest answer they can give.

To get around this legal fear, ask questions like "Have you ever seen this candidate face a challenge? How did they overcome it?" or "Can you tell me about a time this candidate achieved something remarkable?" Questions like this allow you to assess the candidate's character—those key attributes like adaptability, drive, and grit—without getting into anything illegal, immoral, or questionable.

## ASSESSMENT TESTS

When used properly, assessment tests offer a consistent, objective, science-backed method of screening candidates. They are typically easy and low cost to administer, and they can look for the specific attributes you want.

In 1917, the US Army pioneered cognitive (IQ) testing in applicant screening during World War I, which was the largest hiring event the world had ever seen. The Army had little time to determine each applicant's capabilities because the war demanded soldiers immediately. As a solution, they decided to take the IQ testing being used in schools and apply it to job placement. It worked, and the world learned from that experiment. Prior to World War I, almost no companies were screening applicants using intelligence or personality assessment tests. Today, it is common for companies to use assessment tests in the hiring process.

Some of the most common tests used today are Hogan Assessments, like Leader Basis and Candidate Comparison. These tests are designed to be *pre-hire* assessments. In addition to providing information about a candidate's organizational fit, potential strengths, potential concerns, and innate ability to be a leader, these tests also give interview tips, including sample questions and areas to further probe.

Picking the right assessment test isn't easy. It's best to do your research or get advice from a trained professional, or you might end up buying a sales pitch instead of a useful assessment test. To get the most out of an assessment test, you must be thoughtful in choosing which one you use, as discussed in chapter 6, "Know Thyself."

For bulk-hiring of some lower-level roles, assessment tests can be a cost-effective way to screen out those candidates least likely to succeed, similar to the minimum-requirements gate. This method can work well, but only when properly designed by qualified industrial-organizational psychologists. While this method has a clear ROI, if you try to do this yourself, you could easily end up eliminating qualified candidates, not to mention risking being on the wrong end of a legal battle.

For more senior roles, especially leadership positions, assessment tests should be a source of additional information, not a screening tool. It's similar to how Special Operations used multiple types of information or intelligence, a practice termed "layering intelligence," during the Global War on Terrorism. They used multiple forms of intelligence, such as signals intelligence (SIGINT), which primarily involved the interception of signals, imagery intelligence (IMINT), intel gathering from satellite and aerial photography, and human intelligence (HUMINT) from the local populaces. HUMINT is often unreliable and hinges on the reliability of the source, which is subject to human bias and can sometimes be distorted due to outright lying. Nevertheless, it was valuable intel when used in conjunction with SIGINT or IMINT, as it could corroborate information and give broader context. Any source of information alone would have been insufficient; *multiple* were needed.

In the same way, assessment tests can provide valuable information, but they only reveal *part* of the picture. For this reason, use these tools in context. For your senior roles, these tests are best used to substantiate and validate your subjective assessments of talent in interviews and observation, not make your hiring decisions for you.

One company we worked with at EF Overwatch used an aptitude, motivation, and personality assessment to weed out candidates. Our veterans, despite being high performers, were all scoring very low on the test and thus being eliminated from the hiring process. Curious, Mike took the test for himself. His score? Just 57 percent—a failing grade.

Now, obviously, we're a little biased when it comes to Mike, but the man is a decorated Navy SEAL, finished number one out of almost every military school he attended, was a 2017 *Poets & Quants* National MBA to Watch, and has proven his worth as a leader in some of the most complex and chaotic environments in the world again and again. He arguably falls into the high talent category. This company had even specifically hired him for his subject-matter expertise in the leadership realm. And yet, based on their assessment test, if he applied as a candidate, they wouldn't hire him as a leader in their organization. His application would have ended up on the chopping block, just like all the veterans before him.

If you're not careful, relying too heavily on an assessment test can mean missing out on talent. It can also mean inadvertently hiring low-potential candidates because people often know how to game tests. So be cautious about relying too heavily on assessments.

Ultimately, if a test alone could tell you who would be a good hire, we wouldn't have such a talent crisis in this country. Talent is unique and often looks different from what you'd expect. That means it also tests differently than what you'd expect. Assessment tools are great for identifying patterns and traits shared by the high performers of your company and can be used to quickly weed out the riskiest applicants for some entry-level positions. They can also highlight red flags and areas that may require more investigation. But for most positions, they should be used more holistically, as a means of better understanding the candidate, not as a screening tool.

## SOME WARNINGS

If you create a multivariate assessment process with pressure testing built in, you will already be leaps and bounds ahead of many companies. To further increase your competitive advantage, heed these warnings:

- Beware of outsourcing.
- Don't be arrogant.
- Avoid nepotism.
- Reduce bias.
- Don't expect perfection.

## BEWARE OF OUTSOURCING

Building an effective talent acquisition program can be overwhelming. Sometimes you *need* external help. We're not saying that you must avoid outsourcing entirely. EF Overwatch, as an executive search and recruiting firm, is an outsourcing solution, so of course, we believe that outsourcing can be an immensely valuable strategy. You can absolutely outsource to *find talent*, but you should not outsource *the hiring decision itself or the process.*

When you outsource your assessment and selection process, you are relinquishing control over the most important strategic advantage your company has. Some recruiting firms are only interested in making hires as quickly as possible so that they can get paid. So if you are going to outsource, you must do your research and be confident in who you are trusting with this critical piece of your business.

To select a good outsourcing partner, search for organizations that align with the principles of this book. Essentially, you want to use outsourcing to help you execute the techniques, not the strategy of talent acquisition. The strategy must come from you.

## DON'T BE ARROGANT

Arrogance can cost you valuable talent. That's what happened when George interviewed with—and then turned down—one of the largest and most recognizable tech firms in the world.

After George completed three initial phone/video interviews, the company flew him out to their headquarters for an entire day of interviewing. The first three interviews in the morning went very well. The interviewers challenged George's brainpower in a good way. They wanted to know how he thought, and he appreciated that, seeing it as an indicator of a strong talent mindset at the company. Lunch went well too, and up to this point, it was George's best experience ever interviewing. He was impressed and already thinking about how he could adopt similar practices. Then he had his seventh and final interview.

This time, the tone of the interview was markedly different and excessively snobbish. Since George had made it this far in the process, he'd already proven himself as a viable leader. If he didn't have the key ingredients needed to succeed at this firm, he would have been eliminated already. Yet his interviewer, the person who would be his boss's boss if he took the job, took an arrogant attitude with a haughty tone of "Why would we hire *you?*" The question wasn't inquisitive or a challenge for George to sell himself. It was perfunctory and misaligned to the process George had been through thus far.

Before George left for the airport to fly home, the coordinator told him that he'd done really well and that they expected to make him an offer. But the last interview had left a sour taste in George's mouth. He wanted to work for leaders with humility, who wanted to continually improve the organization and the individuals around them. When he landed in Phoenix for his layover, much to the surprise of the tech firm, he called the coordinator and withdrew himself from consideration. He was politically correct in his explanation for why, but ultimately, the true reason was that he didn't want to work with or for arrogant people. People choose bosses more than they choose specific roles. This is the power of leadership—people want to work for great leaders.

If you want the best talent at your organization, you can't be arrogant. You might think you have the pick of the litter, but talented people have a lot of options. They aren't going to tolerate arrogance or disrespect, or if they do, it will be short-lived. They will simply take their talents someplace where they are valued and leadership is strong. Interviewers should always be respectful and professional—remember, they are representing your company. Never forget that the candidate is interviewing you and your company at the same time you are interviewing them.

## AVOID NEPOTISM

Nepotism is relatively nonexistent in the Special Operations assessment and selection process. Regardless of sociodemographic factors, who someone may know, or whether their father served in Special Operations, everyone must go through the assessment and selection process to earn a place in the organization. Many SEALS' sons will attempt to follow in their fathers' footsteps, but if they don't make it through BUD/S, that's the end of the story. There are no familial ties that result in special exceptions.

Once an individual makes it into the SOF community, further advancement is not possible without a good reputation. Reputation and nepotism are different, though. Reputation is based on an individual's character and performance. Nepotism, on the other hand, rewards people based on personal relationships. Being respected by one's peers, leaders, and team is an indicator of high potential; being someone's friend or family member is not. Making hiring decisions based on nepotism shows a lack of talent mindset and will not sit well with those within your organization. Reputations and respect must be earned, not given. Simply giving someone a senior-level title does not give them the needed character, skills, or respect to perform well in that role.

In addition to eliminating nepotism, you must take measures to reduce bias as much as possible.

## REDUCE BIAS

Bias is the enemy of accuracy. "We all bring biases to the table," says Brian Decker. "In any selection process, if you don't account for bias, you're going to select in your own image." Bias is unavoidable, and there are a number of cognitive biases that arise in assessment and selection, including ingroup bias, the halo effect, confirmation bias, the one-trick-pony fallacy, and groupthink.

Ingroup bias is the tendency to give preferential treatment to people we perceive as being part of our group. Studies have shown that, in betting, people will bet on their own group, even if there is no reason to do so. If the odds are the same or even slightly in favor of the opposing group, people will still bet on their own group for no reason other than the fact that they are in that group.[21] Essentially, people think, "If I'm in a group, that group is better." We are all a part of any number of different groups. In hiring, ingroup bias means that we might give preferential treatment to people who are our same gender or race, who attended the same school as us, who earned the same degree, who worked at the same company, or who simply support the same sports team as us.

The halo effect is the tendency to allow a positive impression of a person in one area to influence your opinion in another area. Say a candidate worked for a prestigious company. Due to the halo effect, that single positive indicator makes you more likely to think positively of the person as a whole, blinding you to potential red flags. As an example of the halo effect in interviewing, if somebody answers the first few questions well, you may decide that they are a quality candidate and thus give them higher ratings on the remaining questions; conversely, if they answer poorly, you may decide they are not a good candidate and rate them more harshly on the following questions.

Connected to the halo effect is confirmation bias—the tendency to interpret information in a way that supports your preconceived beliefs. If you decide early on that a person would be a good hire, because perhaps the person graduated from an Ivy League school, you will only pay attention to the information that supports your belief. Confirmation bias can work in the opposite direction too:

---

21 H. Tajfel, "Experiments in Intergroup Discrimination," *Scientific American* 223, no. 2 (1970): 96–102; Henri Tajfel, M. G. Billig, R. P. Bundy, and Claude Flament, "Social Categorization and Intergroup Behaviour," European Journal of Social Psychology 1, no. 2 (1971): 149–178.

if you believe a person would be a bad hire, you will only see the negative information that reinforces that belief.

The one-trick-pony fallacy—our term for the tendency to think people can be good at only one thing—is another harmful bias. We have a tendency to put people in boxes. If they are extremely good or specialized in one area, we reduce them to that one thing. For instance, we wouldn't expect that a famous baseball player would also be an excellent piano player or accountant. In reality, people who are exceptionally knowledgeable or skilled at one thing and one thing only are rare. In general, if someone has figured out how to be good at one thing, they have the underlying character needed to become good at many other things. Plus, many skills transfer from one area to another. For example, many chemists are talented cooks because they understand how ingredients go together.

The one-trick-pony fallacy is most often an issue when it comes to a candidate's experience. Because we think people are good at only one thing, we have difficulty translating experience from one industry to another. This is part of why Special Operations veterans don't always receive a fair evaluation. Operators are seen as warriors and warriors alone. People underestimate operators' ability to thrive in a different setting. A civilian hiring manager once told us that a Navy SEAL "would rather gouge his eyes out than work in a desk job." We mentioned her comment to a SEAL, and he said, "Where does she think we do work?" Yes, SEALS spend time on the battle-field, but they also have desk jobs. They have meetings, PowerPoint presentations, and performance reviews, just like in any company.

Combined, ingroup bias, the halo effect, confirmation bias, and the one-trick-pony fallacy lead us to hire people according to a specific, limited mold. Typically, that mold is a reflection of ourselves. We are drawn to those people who look and think like us.

While people who are similar to us might be likable, that's not a good reason to hire someone. As Soichiro Honda said, "If you hire only those people you understand, the company will never get people better than you are. Always remember that you often find outstanding people among those you don't particularly like."[22]

Companies are most successful when they contain a diversity of thought. By hiring people with diverse backgrounds, strengths, and thought processes, you increase the possibility for innovation and the detection of errors. If everyone thinks the same way, you limit what your company can accomplish. General Patton said, "If everyone is thinking alike, then somebody isn't thinking."

One of the best ways to reduce bias is to train your hiring team in the unconscious cognitive biases they are likely to encounter. If they are aware of the potential for bias, they will be more likely to recognize it in action, resulting in more accurate assessments.

Another effective way to reduce bias is to choose your hiring team thoughtfully, as discussed in the previous chapter. By having multiple individuals from different departments and levels involved in hiring, you can counteract a single individual's bias.

Creating a team for hiring can limit many biases, but it also introduces a new bias: groupthink, or herd mentality. When in a group, we tend to seek harmony by modifying our behaviors and thoughts in alignment with the group. To combat this, keep

22 "The Philosophy of Mr. Honda," Honda, http://www.hondaresearch.com/values.php.

assessments separate throughout the process using something similar to a secret ballot. Research shows that if someone writes down their thoughts before talking with others, it's more likely to be what they actually think. If they talk to others first, their opinion is skewed. Each member of the hiring team should score candidates independently, keeping written notes and observations. Until all the steps are complete, the hiring team should not share notes or talk to one another about candidates (unless they're on a panel interview together). Once the independent observations are complete, then everyone should gather for a final discussion.

## DON'T EXPECT PERFECTION

Perfection is an unattainable goal. There is no perfect candidate, and there is no perfect hiring process.

When assessing candidates, don't get hung up on anomalies. For instance, say a candidate doesn't demonstrate good leadership in a one-on-one role-play exercise, but they do demonstrate it in a group exercise, as well as in their interviews and on an assessment test. The clear pattern here is good leadership. The one role-play exercise is likely an anomaly. It may be worth investigating further, but don't let a single mistake eliminate an otherwise talented candidate.

Part of the purpose of a multivariate assessment is to ensure that anomalies are not overly weighted in selection. Don't expect a candidate to be perfect in every aspect of the assessment process. Instead, look for patterns—common themes across the different assessments. Patterns are hard to fake and highly predictive of the future, so they're a good guide.

Just as you can't expect perfection from your candidates, you can't expect perfection from your hiring team, either. To create a culture of innovation and continuous improvement, you have to allow for failures. "You're never going to eliminate all the false positives or all the false negatives," says Tom Lokar. No matter how skilled the hiring team, they will sometimes hire candidates that turn out to be a disappointment. That's okay. Learn from that. Your goal should be progress, not perfection. Every time you learn and improve your process, you're building a bigger competitive advantage.

While you shouldn't expect perfection, you should still strive for improvement. You should always be working to better your hiring process, and you do that through a feedback loop.

## FEEDBACK LOOP

A hiring process is not truly complete until it has a feedback loop to assess its effectiveness. Very few companies go back to determine whether they made the right hiring decision, but this is key to improving your hiring process.

To create a feedback loop, document the hiring process thoroughly. Keep all the notes and scorecards for each candidate you hire. Do early check-ins with new hires and their managers. Funnel that data back to the recruiting group and those who participated in the actual screening process for that candidate. The next time the company does formal employee reviews, identify which new employees are performing well and which ones are not. Then return to the notes and documentation from the hiring process. Look for clues and patterns—anything that might indicate what in the hiring process led to the good hires and what led to the poor hires. "It's important to see who was successful and who wasn't," says Tracy, "because it hones your ability to identify talent."

The hiring team needs to be personally involved in this feedback loop. As Tracy says, that way they will know, "Oh, that little whisper in the back of my mind about whether this person was going to fit or whether they were exaggerating their ability, now I see I should have listened to that." Tracy continues, "You have to do closed-loop learning to be able to improve your hit rate. It makes you a much better recruiter, and all it takes is a willingness to go back and look at who you hired and how they fared in the organization."

Aside from tracking new hires' performance, the best way to gain feedback on your hiring process is to ask the people who go through it. At the end of assessment and selection, distribute a short survey to all the candidates, both the ones who received a job offer and those who didn't. Ask them what they think of the screening process and the company's communication.

Obviously, some unselected candidates may give negative feedback out of bitterness, but others will provide valuable information. If there is a pattern of negative feedback from unselected candidates, you may have a problem with your hiring process. Ideally, your hiring process should be a positive experience for both those who are selected and those who are not. As Rich Diviney says, "How you treat people who may not get the chance to work for you speaks to the level of competency and professionalism of an organization. If you are able to respectfully articulate to somebody why they might not be a good fit for your organization or your team, it shows deep thought, care, and accountability across all levels."

The biggest argument we hear from companies about feedback loops is that they simply do not have the time to implement them. Brian Decker argues, "You don't have the time not to." Without a feedback loop, it will take you far more time to refine your process and make it as effective as it can be.

Building a more effective assessment and selection program will put you ahead of the competition, but the war for talent does not stop there. In fact, that's where the longer war begins. As we will discuss in the next chapter, you have to continually develop your talent to cultivate leaders within your organization.

## KEY TAKEAWAYS

- The hiring process can include interviews, observation of candidates, and assessment tests. To be most effective, use a multivariate assessment process, where multiple assessment strategies are used, including a mix of subjective and objective measures.
- Pressure testing is critical. Under stress and adversity, true character is revealed.
- Interview questions should be standardized and aligned to specific character attributes, with scenario-based and behavioral questions being best. To add pressure, give candidates challenges, like case studies, during the interview and push them out of their comfort zone.
- Perhaps the best way to evaluate behavior is to observe candidates in action. You can do this using role play,

group exercises, covert observation, or all of these together in an assessment center.

- Your hiring process reflects back on your company. Don't be arrogant, and try to avoid nepotism and bias.
- No hiring process is perfect, but with a feedback loop, you can continually refine your hiring process into an effective tool for talent acquisition.

A US Special Forces Operational Detachment Alpha (ODA) commander leads a combined US and Afghan Special Operations Task Force during nighttime combat operations in a contested region of southern Afghanistan. This leader has positioned himself on a rooftop, exposed to enemy fire, to relay a situation report, known as a SITREP, to his chain of command via satellite radio. Commanding troops in combat is one of the most daunting challenges any human can ever face. Any battle-hardened veteran will be quick to tell you, "Combat is the ultimate test of leadership."

*Source: Defense Visual Information Distribution Service / Sgt. Connor Mendez*

# CHAPTER 10

# YOU CAN'T HIRE OR FIRE YOUR WAY TO SUCCESS

Talent acquisition is only one part of a two-variable equation for success:

*Talent + Leadership = Victory*

This is something Mike learned early on in his SEAL career. After BUD/S, Mike checked into Task Unit Charlie, SEAL Team 3. It was his first experience in the SEAL teams, and it would be the worst eight months of his twenty-year career, but also the best lesson he could learn as a young officer. He was about to receive a master class in the differences and effects of bad leadership versus good leadership.

From day one, the two most senior leaders in Task Unit Charlie refused to work together. Their mission was to turn Task Unit

Charlie into a highly effective, versatile, lethal, and cohesive unit prepared for deployment to Iraq. It should have been a relatively simple task, as the forty SEALS assigned to Task Unit Charlie were among the most highly trained soldiers in the US military. Each one had completed SEAL training, and several had multiple combat deployments under their belt.

Task Unit Charlie clearly had the talent but was missing the leadership component. The two senior leaders were unable to check their egos and work together during the combat training. The unit quickly became divided, with two camps emerging. Even Mike eventually chose sides, defying all the leadership training he had received from the Marine Corps.

Mike began to think this was how SEAL teams conducted business—the complete opposite of a "team." It was a toxic environment, and the culture was destructive to any cohesion among the men. The unit failed several training blocks during the unit-level training to deploy to combat. Nobody accepted ownership, instead pointing figures and casting blame on the opposing camp. The weight of the failure fueled the hate between the two camps, creating even more division.

Two months away from deploying overseas, the commanding officer of SEAL Team 3 could no longer ignore the problem and relieved (military lingo for "fired") the two senior members of Task Unit Charlie.

Mike was immediately reassigned to Task Unit Bruiser, located just one office down. The unit, led by Jocko Willink, was one month away from deploying to the worst place in the world at that time—Ramadi, Iraq, in 2006.

Mike had graduated Honor Man (the number one graduate) from almost every military school he'd attended in the Marine Corps and Navy and had built a solid reputation in the Marine Corps Reconnaissance community and throughout the initial SEAL training. He'd even been the "Fire in the Gut" winner in BUD/S, selected by the other students as the person they would most want to follow into combat. Mike had all the *potential* to be a great leader, but the potential had not yet been translated into *performance.*

The command leadership asked Jocko to take Mike on as his assistant operations officer and determine if he was redeemable. Jocko had asked around about Mike and already knew he was capable. Those who worked closely with Mike identified him as a standout leader, marred only by the fact that he had been sucked into the recent leadership failure of Task Unit Charlie.

Over the next eight months, Jocko committed to mentoring and coaching Mike. He continually offered opportunities and set stretch goals to test Mike's abilities and leadership potential. After Mike's second month with Task Unit Bruiser, Jocko promoted him to lead operations officer. A month after that, Jocko assigned him to Delta Platoon as their assistant officer-in-charge, to join them during the pivotal months of the Battle of Ramadi.

Under bad leadership, stuck in a toxic culture, Mike regressed from his reputation, moving in the opposite direction as a leader. Under strong leadership and day-to-day mentorship, his leadership potential accelerated rapidly.

Both Task Unit Charlie and Task Unit Bruiser pulled from the same elite talent pool, all of whom had proven themselves in SEAL training. Both units possessed the same level of talent and had access to the same resources (funding, equipment/gear, and training). *The variables were practically the same*, yet Task Unit Bruiser excelled beyond measure, and Task Unit Charlie crumbled under the weight of the intense training.

*There was one key difference: leadership.* Task Unit Charlie versus Task Unit Bruiser was the perfect test of the effects and impact that good and bad leadership have on an organization. The results of the test were clear: without good leadership, there can be no victory.

If you want to be victorious, you need good leaders, and that requires transforming your high potentials into high performers.

# FROM HIGH POTENTIAL TO HIGH PERFORMER: THE POWER OF CONTINUOUS DEVELOPMENT

This chapter's title—"You Can't Hire or Fire Your Way to Success"— may seem contradictory, considering this book is about the importance of selecting, assessing, and hiring talent. But what also makes SOF truly special is the unwavering and relentless commitment to the development of its talent.

Talent acquisition *is* crucial, but so is talent development. Talent development is the catalyst that transforms a hire from high potential to high performer.

Whole books could be—and have been—written about how to train employees and develop leaders. (One of the best we've seen is *Extreme Ownership: How US Navy SEALS Lead and Win* by Jocko

Willink and Leif Babin.) With just one chapter dedicated to this topic, we will not be providing an exhaustive explanation of how to build an effective training and leadership development program. Rather, we will focus on the *why*, highlighting the dire need to invest in and develop your people.

> *You can have the most effective talent acquisition program in the world, but if you don't properly develop your talent,* ***your company will most likely still fail.***

Far too often, a company will hire a talented candidate whose performance ends up being lackluster. The company chalks it up to a bad hire, fires that person, and starts over again—a costly assumption. There are many reasons someone might not be performing as you expect, and only one of them is a bad hire. Chances are if a talented individual is not performing to standard, it's not their fault; *it's yours.*

There are few off-the-shelf hires that you can onboard and plug into a position with little to no guidance, but the "plug-and-play" mentality is all too common. In reality, once you hire a talented individual, your job has only just begun. People with raw talent have the *potential* to be high performers. It is up to you to give them the resources and feedback to grow into their potential.

From entry-level to C-suite, all members of your team require development to sustain and continually enhance their performance. Talent development cannot be a one-time onboarding procedure; it must be continuous.

This is one of the keys to SOF's success. Some people imagine that after an operator graduates from the initial assessment, selection, and training schoolhouses, like BUD/S or the Q Course, they have completed their training. This couldn't be further from the truth. Whether you spend six years in the SOF community or thirty-five, one thing is certain: the training never stops, no matter what level you serve at.

Mike spent 240 months in the military to reach retirement; 195 were spent training for the 45 months he spent in combat. Over 80 percent of his career was spent training for the 20 percent he spent in combat. From his first day in boot camp until late in his career at a highly specialized and highly selective SEAL Team, he trained every day—from elaborate training scenarios staged with Hollywood-style explosives, to walking the historic battlefield of Gettysburg to learn from past military leaders, to continual assessment and standardized tests.

Though all hires require training, you should pay extra attention to those who show leadership potential. As General Boykin explains, "[The SOF community] goes to great lengths to identify who the future leaders are, the ones that are going to sustain the organization, and we pour into them in a different way than we pour into the other people."

Part of the purpose of training is to teach team members the hard and soft skills necessary to perform in their role, but training is also how you create future leaders, just as Jocko helped build Mike into a leader. Within your training, leadership development should be a top priority because leadership determines success.

## TRAINING, MENTORING, COACHING, AND LEADING BY EXAMPLE

There are four main categories of talent development: training, mentoring, coaching, and leading by example. Here's a breakdown of what each of those terms means, with valuable input from Bill Gardner, Executive Coach and Managing Partner at Noetic Outcomes Consulting:

- *Training* is relaying the knowledge and skills needed to accomplish assigned outcomes: "Here's what you need to know and what you need to be able to do to solve it."

- *Mentoring* is advising someone based on expertise gained from career experiences: "Here's what I did to solve it when I was in your position."

- *Coaching* is asking great questions so the coachee learns to solve their current and future problems: "How will *you* solve it?"

- *Leading by example* is living the company's values and really walking the talk: "Do as I say, *and* do as I do."

# LEADERSHIP DETERMINES SUCCESS

*The most important thing in any organization is leadership. It's always leadership first, because leaders find a way to get things done.*
—Joe DePinto, CEO of 7-Eleven

For essentially as long as the military has existed, leadership has been recognized as the decisive factor on the battlefield. Alexander the Great said, "An army of sheep led by a lion is better than an army of lions led by a sheep." Your leaders have extraordinary levels of impact—as Special Operations Forces are the Tip of the Spear for the military, your leaders are the Tip of the Spear for your organization. An effective leader will guide your organization into the future, while a bad leader can poison it.

In a business, you achieve victory when:

1. **Sales** are up, and you're dominating in your space.
2. **Labor efficiency** is good, leading to manageable costs and appropriate use of resources.
3. **Profits**, as a result of 1 and 2, are growing.
4. **Customer satisfaction** is high, resulting in customer and market-share gains.
5. **Employee engagement/satisfaction** is great, and people work as a **team**. As a result, **retention** is high, and the **culture** is healthy and enjoyable.

6. **Innovation** is part of your culture, and people are quick to adapt to changing conditions. Individually and organizationally, there is a **growth mindset**.

In our opinion, leadership is *the* most critical determinant of achieving victory for a business. Leaders are the ones who drive change and make things happen. So when working to transform high potentials into high performers, it's critical to identify and develop future leaders.

The most effective businesses have true leadership at all levels, from the C-suite down to the assembly line. Tom Lokar says, "It's a universal truth that, at every level, leadership matters." As Bill Schaninger, McKinsey & Company's HR practice leader, says, "A CEO and the board can't be better than their team. It's like being an editor and having a bunch of bad writers." To achieve enterprise-wide excellence in execution, you must have leaders at all levels of the organization, especially within the frontline troops (entry-level employees). If leadership is missing at any level, the organization will not perform to its full potential.

Fortunately, leadership is something that can be taught and developed. "Leaders are made, they are not born," said Vince Lombardi. "They are made by hard effort, which is the price which all of us must pay to achieve any goal that is worthwhile."

While leaders are made and not born, General Boykin points out, "Not everybody can lead, period." Talent is a prerequisite to becoming a leader. Only those individuals with drive, resiliency, adaptability, humility, integrity, effective intelligence, team-ability, curiosity, and emotional strength can be developed and molded into leaders.

To develop effective leaders, you need to start with talent, and to attract talent, you need effective leaders. It's a continual cycle, with one building upon the other, which makes a strong leadership foundation essential.

## BUILD A WORLD-CLASS LEADERSHIP FOUNDATION

A company without a leadership foundation is like a ship without a rudder. Too many companies rush to create a world-class talent acquisition pipeline as if it will be a cure-all for their talent problems, but without a solid leadership foundation in place, it will be impossible to retain talent. Talent has a choice where it chooses to work, and it won't put up with bad leadership.

Not only is bad leadership destructive to cultures, it's *expensive*. Bad leadership leads to employee disengagement and, worse, high attrition. The cost of replacing a salaried employee has been estimated to be six to nine months' salary on average,[23] and Gallup has estimated that disengaged employees cost an organization approximately $3,400 for every $10,000 of salary, or 34 percent, due to tardiness, missed workdays, and decreased productivity.[24]

Building an effective talent pool and running a winning organization requires not just a world-class talent pipeline, but also a world-class leadership foundation.

---

23  Christina Merhar, "Employee Retention—The Real Cost of Losing an Employee," PeopleKeep, February 4, 2016, https://www.peoplekeep.com/blog/bid/312123/employee-retention-the-real-cost-of-losing-an-employee.

24  "Calculating the Cost of Employee Attrition and Disengagement," LinkedIn Learning, https://learning.linkedin.com/content/dam/me/learning/en-us/pdfs/lil-workbook-calculating-cost-of-employee-attrition-and-disengagement.pdf.

Great organizations, like the Special Operations community, take the time to create a universal *leadership foundation*. A leadership foundation, similar to a talent mindset, is a culture and belief that is woven throughout an organization. It provides a common language and common leadership principles from which an organization's people grow, lead, and solve problems. Essentially, your leadership foundation defines what it means to be a good leader within your organization. It tells leaders what standards and values they are expected to embody. It thus provides the framework from which the organization strives for excellence and the means for people to evaluate their progress and improvement as leaders, both individually and collectively as an organization.

The military has long understood the importance of a leadership foundation. With the longest onboarding process of any organization in the world, the military drives home the leadership principles, code of conduct, and core values demanded of its service members. With two to three months of 24/7 leadership development and cultural assimilation, their culture adoption rate is unrivaled in the business world. This process creates a leadership foundation that every Soldier, Marine, Airman, and Sailor speaks, understands, and lives.

This kind of leadership foundation can and should be applied to the business world. Many times, when we work with companies, before we can fix their talent problem, we have to fix their leadership problem. Otherwise, we would simply create a revolving door of talent, where talented individuals are hired into the company but then quickly leave due to a lack of leadership.

The creation of a leadership foundation leads to clear results. In 2014, one of Mike's past mentors, a former Army officer and

Ranger School graduate, assumed the role of president and COO of a healthcare services company, and one of his first acts as president was to build a leadership foundation. He created an onboarding process for all employees, from entry-level to executives. The several-day onboarding process centered around the leadership philosophy and principles set forth in *The US Army Leadership Field Manual*, known as the FM 22-100. Rather than establishing a leadership foundation from scratch, he took a page, or several, from one of the historically best-led organizations in the world, the US Army. With this onboarding, every single member of the company understood the core values and leadership principles they were expected to exhibit in their day-to-day behaviors. More or less, they spoke the same language of leadership, promoting continued personal and organizational growth.

The company experienced unprecedented growth over the next several years, successfully positioning itself as a sole nationwide provider for its specific service. Though the company benefited from an aggressive acquisition strategy, the true strength came from the leadership foundation, which led to stronger leaders at all levels of the organization. The culture of organizational health and leadership made the company a top place to work within its industry. Mike's mentor received Ernst & Young's Entrepreneur of the Year Award within his respective region and industry, the same exact year the company was acquired by a private equity firm for $1 billion.

Leadership matters. Leaders achieve results, no matter the industry. They are the critical determinant of success for a business because they are the ones who transform employees' potential into performance. There is no stronger legacy than that of leadership. But good leadership doesn't appear in organizations by chance. Good leadership is sought out, identified, recruited, trained, and retained by organizations that lead with a talent mindset.

## HOPELESS TO HARDCORE: TURNING B-PLAYERS INTO A-PLAYERS

The greatest lesson any military or business leader can learn is "There are no bad teams, only bad leaders."[25] Even in the worst circumstances, it is possible to transform a bad team into a winning unit through exceptional leadership. For proof, look no further than Colonel David Hackworth and the transformation of US Army, 4th Battalion, 39th Infantry.

During the Vietnam War, Hackworth (then a lieutenant colonel) inherited what the brigade commander described as the "worst battalion I've seen in twenty-six years of service."[26] Hackworth took that hopeless battalion, which suffered the Army's highest casualty rate, and transformed it into one of the most lethal and effective military units of the Vietnam War.

---

25 Jocko Willink and Leif Babin, *Extreme Ownership: How US Navy SEALS Lead and Win* (New York: St. Martin's Press, 2017), 49.
26 David H. Hackworth and Eilhys England, *Steel My Soldiers' Hearts: The Hopeless to Hardcore Transformation of US Army, 4th Battalion, 39th Infantry, Vietnam* (New York: Touchstone, 2002), 8.

"The whole base smelled of raw shit and rotting morale," Hackworth wrote in his account, *Steel My Soldiers' Hearts*. "Toilet paper blew across the chopper pad, machine-gun ammo was buried in mud, and troops wandered around like zombies, their weapons gone red with rust. These were the sloppiest American soldiers I'd ever seen, bar none. Unkempt, unwashed, unshaven, their uniforms ragged and dirty, hippie beads dangling alongside their dog tags, their helmets covered with graffiti."[27]

Hackworth immediately got to work to transform the poorly led and undisciplined unit into a capable organization. His first order was for the soldiers to build better fighting positions—no easy task in the jungle. He also implemented strict protocols of discipline in phases, adding one new requirement at a time, like shaving every day, wearing helmets on the firebase, and always being in camouflage when on operations. He also brought back saluting and branded the battalion as "Hardcore Recondos" (a nickname that would stick) to build esprit de corps.

At first, many of the soldiers hated him for his strict requirements, but the extra discipline soon produced results. Under Hackworth's leadership, the battalion's casualty numbers declined, and they executed more damage against the enemy.

---

27  Hackworth and England, *Steel My Soldiers' Hearts*, 9.

Aside from producing results, Hackworth also balanced his tough love with deep devotion to his men. He regularly braved enemy fire to reach wounded soldiers, direct operations, and provide fire support and even joined in the fighting himself when needed. During his tenure as commanding officer of the Hardcore Recondos, Hackworth was awarded five Silver Stars and a Distinguished Service Cross. (Total, throughout his entire career, Hackworth received ten Silver Stars, two Distinguished Service Crosses, and eight Purple Hearts.)

Hackworth is a testament to the power of a single inspirational leader. With effective leadership, you can upgrade your talent, turning B-players into A-players.

## THE LEGACY OF LEADERSHIP

When you become a leader, your impact is no longer limited to what you can accomplish individually; every person you lead becomes an extension of you, creating an exponential impact.

When the two of us look back at our careers and our time in the military, we feel fortunate to have received world-class mentorship and leadership development. We've learned from some of our nation's most prominent leaders. Mike would not be the leader he is today without Ground Force Commanders like Jocko Willink and Special Operations senior enlisted leaders and officers whose names we cannot mention for security purposes. Likewise,

George would not be such an effective leader without key mentors like Major General Sidney Shachnow, Brigadier General Rodney Johnson, and Lieutenant Colonel David Bradley, as well as Tracy Keogh, Don Robertson, and Tom Lokar, whose positive influence can clearly be seen in this book.

Leadership, both good and bad, creates a chain reaction. All the people who were instrumental to our development and maturation as leaders had their own mentors and influences. Jocko, for instance, came up under some highly respected and skilled leaders in the SEAL teams, while the two senior leaders in Task Unit Charlie were a product of bad prior SEAL mentors. Our mentors passed on the lessons they'd learned to us, and today, we are passing those same lessons on to others.

With the right leaders in place, you will create an unbroken chain of excellence throughout your organization. You will no longer need to look externally for leadership hires, because you will have already home-grown the leaders you need. General Boykin considers this a litmus test for the quality of your company's leadership development. "If you're hiring for a leadership role and can't find somebody internally, then your leadership development needs significant work," he says. If the Green Berets need a new commander, they're not going to hire a Fortune 500 CEO for the job; they're going to promote a Green Beret. If they don't have a qualified Green Beret, then something has gone very wrong.

For middle- to upper-level management positions, the goal is to be promoting from within. (The rare exception is when your organization is branching out in a new direction and you require unique skills that are not currently present in the organization.)

The stronger your leadership foundation and leadership development, the greater the degree to which you'll be able to promote from within.

Hiring from within has four major benefits: (1) It helps your bottom line, as internal hires are cheaper than external hires. (2) It's more efficient. Because homegrown leaders are already steeped in the leadership foundation and culture of your company, they have a much faster ramp-up time. (3) You get better quality, as homegrown leaders understand the company and its needs in a way that external hires typically don't. Plus, you trained them yourself, so you know you're getting exactly what you want. (4) Hiring from within allows you to engage in effective succession planning, which is one of the key traits that has led to SOF becoming a world-class organization.

With a legacy of leadership, each new generation of homegrown leaders stands upon the backs of those who came before them, allowing them to push farther and achieve more than they ever could on their own.

## A TRUE TALENT MINDSET

Remember: the most critical step in winning the talent war is developing a *talent mindset*—deep belief that leadership and human capital are the most important competitive advantage your company can have.

If you truly believe that leadership and human capital are your greatest competitive advantage, you won't stop with the hiring process. You will continue to invest in and develop your people, creating an unbroken chain of excellence. That's what good leaders do. That's how great organizations are formed.

The training and leadership development opportunities you provide your employees reveal the truth of your talent mindset. You might be able to attract candidates with talk of a talent mindset, but if you want them to stay, you need to show your employees that you truly value talent by helping them to grow into their potential.

It starts with you. If you demonstrate exemplary leadership, others will follow. Practice a talent mindset. Mentor and coach your key leaders. Put in the time and effort to develop your people into something great, and a great organization will emerge.

## KEY TAKEAWAYS

- Leadership determines success; but leaders must be identified, recruited, acquired, trained, and retained through a *talent mindset.*
- Building talent is a two-phase process: talent acquisition and talent development.
- If you lack training and leadership development, your organization will fail, even if you have a great talent acquisition process.
- Leadership development is a never-ending process. People can always grow and improve, so you must never stop training, coaching, and mentoring them.
- Exceptional leaders who set the example through their actions inspire others to greatness.
- **Talent + Leadership = Victory**

# AFTER-ACTION REVIEW

Assess. Select. Develop. Lead.

This is the winning formula for victory in war and business. Today, talent extends beyond a competitive advantage to a *necessity*. "We live in a total VUCA [volatility, uncertainty, complexity, ambiguity] environment right now," says Joe DePinto, CEO of 7-Eleven. "Ultimately, it is all about talent. If you didn't have the talent before, you might have been able to squeak through. Today, if you don't have it, you lose."

The world is changing at the most rapid pace we've seen. Every year, thousands of businesses fail to evolve at the same pace and close their doors forever. Either you adapt, or you die. New technology is emerging, and greater automation is coming. Right now, a new technology could be in development that might make your entire industry obsolete. There is no telling what kinds of problems your business will face five, ten, and twenty years from now. If you want your company to survive and thrive, you need to focus on the one resource that gets better every year: people. The only way to prepare for the unknown is to fill your company with talent—people who will be able to face whatever comes and find a way through, under, or around it.

Talent is the answer. Talent is universal and eternal, and talent wins every time. It climbs over obstacles and delivers results. It finds a way to victory.

No matter how much technology or the workplace changes, talent is the one constant. You need people with the drive to break through walls to accomplish the mission. The grit to get back up after being knocked down. The adaptability to constantly evolve, innovate, and problem-solve. The humility to be a leader and a team player, to put the team and the mission of the company before themselves. The ethics to do not only what is legal, but what is right. The contextual intelligence to apply their knowledge with situational appropriateness. Most important, the talent and character to step up and lead.

If you've committed to this journey to develop an effective talent acquisition and development function, *congratulations!* It won't happen overnight, but we trust that we have provided you with the foundational principles and strategies to succeed. You don't have to do it alone, though. If you need additional resources, whether it's assessing your current team, developing a roadmap, hiring the right leadership, or other resources, we are here for you, bringing more than thirty years of experience and execution to the table. Contact us at *www.thetalentwar.com* or *www.efoverwatch.com*.

The most important thing is to make an unwavering commitment to fighting this war. If you don't know how to hire well for the jobs you can see now, you have no hope of hiring well for the jobs of tomorrow, the jobs that have not even been invented yet. If you're not bold, if you're not aggressive with a full-on mindset for talent, you're going to lose, and you're going to lose big.

On the other hand, if you attack the problem of talent with the seriousness it deserves, you will gain an edge over your competitors. As CHRO Tom Lokar says, "Why is talent so important? Because it can change the business trajectory. Few things can change the trajectory like building a great team." The advantage will be small at first, but the more you operate from a talent mindset, the more your advantage will increase. It's like building a retirement nest egg. You invest a small amount at a time, and over time, with compounded interest, the money grows and grows, increasing exponentially. By investing in talent, you can transform your entire company.

The Special Operations community is one of the world's most effective talent magnets. In this book, we've guided you through SOF principles on talent acquisition and development that you can apply to your business. Now it's time to turn words into action, it is time to lead. Identify the talent you want, attract it, select it, and cultivate it. That's how great organizations win on talent. And when you win on talent, you get the people and leaders you need to win the war.

**Talent wins.**

# ACKNOWLEDGMENTS

## GEORGE

First, to my wife, Christina, my biggest fan and unwavering supporter who helped bring this idea to life and who helped with editing, wording, and flow. To my family—Kelsey, Mitchell, Russell, Alli, Michael, Noah, and soon-to-arrive grandson.

To my Talent Acquisition leadership team, who are an absolute privilege to work with—Amy Rawlings, Jodie Sweeney, Karli Waldon, Suzie Jimenez, and Miranda Haywood. Thank you for your encouragement and patience as we transformed Talent Acquisition.

To my HR leadership team: Laurie O'Brien, an amazing CHRO; Karen Clark, the standard for HR business partners and my partner in crime; and Emilie McLaughlin, who truly knows that bringing in talent is only the beginning of the journey.

# MIKE

To my beautiful wife, Jordan; my children, Camryn and Caden; my entire family; and all my brothers- and sisters-in-arms who I had the privilege to serve with—you are my purpose for being.

---

This book was made possible through the contributions of countless military and business leaders who share a passion, probably better described as a healthy obsession, for leadership and building winning organizations through the strategic acquisition and development of talent.

- Dr. Josh Cotton—Industrial-Organizational Psychologist and Talent Acquisition Specialist with Honeywell
- Lieutenant Commander Jocko Willink (USN, Ret.)—CEO/ Founder of Echelon Front, author of multiple *New York Times* best-selling books, and retired SEAL
- Lieutenant Commander Leif Babin—COO/Founder of Echelon Front, author of multiple *New York Times* best-selling books, and former SEAL
- Joe DePinto—CEO of 7-Eleven, West Point graduate, and former US Army Officer
- Lieutenant General Jerry Boykin (USA, Ret.)—Executive Vice President of Family Research Council and former Commander of US Army Special Operations Command (USASOC)
- Tracy Keogh—CHRO of Hewlett-Packard

- Lieutenant Colonel Brian Decker (USA, Ret.)—Director of Player Development for the Indianapolis Colts and former US Army Special Forces Assessment and Selection (SFAS) Commander
- Don Robertson—CHRO of Northwestern Mutual
- Tom Lokar—former CHRO of Mitel
- Bill Gardner—Executive Coach and Managing Partner at Noetic Outcomes Consulting
- Commander Rich Diviney (USN, Ret.)—former Assessment and Selection Commander for a highly selective SEAL Team and retired Navy SEAL
- Colonel Carroll Greene (USAF, Ret.)—prior Command Psychologist at multiple USSOCOM units
- Master Chief Jason Tuschen (USN, Ret.)—Co-founder/CEO of Randori Inc. and former SEAL Command Master Chief
- Admiral Alex Krongard (USN, Ret.)—Managing Director of DC Advisory and retired SEAL Admiral
- Lieutenant Colonel Perry Blackburn (USA, Ret)—retired US Army Special Forces Officer
- David Cochran—Executive Vice President of Colliers International
- EF Overwatch team—Trey Holder, Mike Bajema, Noah Nuñez, and Will Sharman
- Echelon Front team—JP Dinnell, David Berke, Jason Gardner, Steve Ward, Jamie Cochran, Jenn Tarantino, Lynn Ortega, Codey Gant, Kaui Mayural, and Ben Duff
- Countless other business leaders and Special Operations leaders from the Air Force CCT and PJ, Army Special Forces,

TF-160th, 75th Ranger Regiment, Joint Special Operations Command, MARSOC, and the Navy SEAL communities who cannot be mentioned due to personal or security reasons

Lastly, we would like to thank Kelsey Adams for her patience and mentorship throughout this process. We could not have written this book without her assistance and eagerly look forward to working on the next one.

# EFOVERWATCH

## A DIFFERENT SOURCE OF EXCEPTIONAL LEADERS

www.efoverwatch.com
info@efoverwatch.com

Follow us at:
www.thetalentwar.com